I0625202

Fulfillment

Unlock the Secrets to Lasting Happiness, Purpose, and Success: A Step-by-Step Guide to Achieving True Fulfillment in Life - The Ultimate Self-Help Handbook!

Lance P. Richards

Fulfillment: Unlock the Secrets to Lasting Happiness, Purpose, and Success: A Step-by-Step Guide to Achieving True Fulfillment in Life - The Ultimate Self-Help Handbook!

Table of Contents

01: Introduction: Understanding Fulfillment

What is fulfillment? It's a word that's thrown around a lot, especially in the self-help industry. We're constantly told that we should strive for fulfillment, that it's the key to happiness and success. But what does it really mean to be fulfilled?

At its core, fulfillment is about feeling content and satisfied with your life. It's about having a sense of purpose and meaning, and feeling like you're making a positive impact in the world. Fulfillment is not just about achieving external goals, like making more money or getting a promotion at work. It's about living a life that feels meaningful and purposeful to you, regardless of what society or others may think.

Unfortunately, many of us struggle to find fulfillment in our lives. We may feel stuck in our careers, unfulfilled in our relationships, or lost when it comes to our sense of purpose. We may find ourselves constantly chasing after external goals, hoping that achieving them will finally bring us the fulfillment we're seeking. But often, even when we achieve these goals, we're left feeling empty and unfulfilled.

01: INTRODUCTION: UNDERSTANDING FULFILLMENT

So how do we find true fulfillment in our lives? That's the question this book aims to answer. Over the course of the next several chapters, we'll explore the key elements of fulfillment, and provide you with practical tools and strategies for achieving it.

We'll start by looking at the importance of self-awareness, and how it's the foundation for all personal growth and fulfillment. We'll then explore the power of mindset, and how your thoughts and beliefs can either propel you forward or hold you back from achieving your goals.

Next, we'll dive into the importance of setting meaningful goals that align with your values and purpose. We'll also explore how to overcome common obstacles and setbacks that may arise along the way.

Throughout the book, we'll also focus on the importance of relationships and connection in achieving fulfillment. We'll explore how to cultivate healthy, fulfilling relationships with both yourself and others, and how to build a supportive community that will help you thrive.

Ultimately, this book is about unlocking the secrets to lasting happiness, purpose, and success. It's about helping you create a life that feels truly fulfilling, in every sense of the word. Whether you're struggling to find direction in your life, feeling unfulfilled in your career, or simply looking to take your life to the next level, the strategies and tools in this book will help you get there.

So let's get started. It's time to unlock the secrets to true fulfillment and create a life that feels deeply satisfying and purposeful.

02: The Science of Happiness and Fulfillment

Introduction

Happiness and fulfillment are two of the most sought-after human experiences. They are the reasons we work hard, strive to achieve our goals, and pursue our passions. Yet, for many people, happiness and fulfillment can seem elusive and difficult to attain. In this chapter, we will explore the science of happiness and fulfillment and uncover the secrets to achieving these states of being.

Understanding Happiness

Before we dive into the science of happiness and fulfillment, let's take a closer look at what happiness actually is. Happiness is a positive emotional state characterized by feelings of pleasure, contentment, and satisfaction. It can be triggered by a variety of factors, such as achieving a goal, spending time with loved ones, or simply enjoying a beautiful day.

However, happiness is not a permanent state of being. It is a fleeting emotion that comes and goes. That's why it's important to understand that happiness is not the ultimate goal of life. Instead, it's a byproduct of living a fulfilling life.

What is Fulfillment?

Fulfillment is the feeling of satisfaction and happiness that comes from living a purposeful and meaningful life. It's about feeling content with who you are, what you do, and the impact you have on the world around you.

Fulfillment is a more sustainable and long-lasting state of being than happiness. It's not just about feeling good in the moment, but about having a deep sense of satisfaction with your life overall.

The Science of Happiness and Fulfillment

Over the past few decades, researchers have been studying happiness and fulfillment in an effort to better understand what drives these states of being. Here are some of the key findings from their research:

Relationships Matter

One of the most consistent findings in the science of happiness is that relationships are essential for our well-being. In fact, studies have shown that having strong social connections is one of the biggest predictors of happiness and fulfillment.

Money Isn't Everything

Contrary to popular belief, money does not necessarily buy happiness. While having enough money to meet basic needs is important, beyond that, more money does not necessarily lead to more happiness.

Gratitude is Key

Practicing gratitude has been shown to be a powerful way to increase happiness and fulfillment. Studies have found that people who regularly practice gratitude report higher levels of well-being and are less likely to experience negative emotions like envy and resentment.

Purpose and Meaning Drive Fulfillment

Having a sense of purpose and meaning in life is essential for experiencing fulfillment. Studies have found that people who have a clear sense of purpose are more likely to experience positive emotions, have stronger social connections, and have a greater sense of overall well-being.

Mindfulness and Self-Awareness are Essential

Being mindful and self-aware can also contribute to happiness and fulfillment. Mindfulness practices, such as meditation, have been shown to reduce stress, increase positive emotions, and improve overall well-being.

Helping Others Helps Ourselves

Finally, research has shown that helping others can be a powerful way to increase our own happiness and fulfillment. Volunteering, donating to charity, or simply helping a friend or family member in need can all contribute to a greater sense of purpose and meaning in life.

Putting it All Together: Achieving Lasting Happiness and Fulfillment

So, how can we apply these findings to our own lives and achieve lasting happiness and fulfillment? Here are some key steps to follow:

Cultivate Strong Relationships

Invest in your relationships with family, friends, and loved ones. Make time for meaningful connections and prioritize building and maintaining strong social connections.

Focus on Purpose and Meaning

Identify your values and what gives your life purpose and meaning. Make sure that your goals and activities align with these values and work towards achieving them.

Practice Gratitude

Make a habit of practicing gratitude on a regular basis. This could be as simple as keeping a gratitude journal or taking a few minutes each day to reflect on the things you're thankful for.

Be Mindful and Self-Aware

Develop mindfulness practices, such as meditation, to help you become more self-aware and present in the moment. This can help reduce stress and increase positive emotions.

Help Others

Look for opportunities to help others, whether it's through

volunteering, donating to charity, or simply helping a friend in need. This can give you a sense of purpose and meaning, as well as increase your own feelings of happiness and fulfillment.

Embrace Challenges

Finally, don't be afraid to embrace challenges and pursue new opportunities. Growth and learning are essential for achieving fulfillment, so don't shy away from new experiences and challenges.

Conclusion

Achieving lasting happiness and fulfillment is a journey, not a destination. It requires consistent effort and a commitment to personal growth and well-being. By cultivating strong relationships, focusing on purpose and meaning, practicing gratitude, being mindful and self-aware, helping others, and embracing challenges, you can unlock the secrets to true fulfillment in life. So, take the first step today and start your journey towards a more fulfilling and happy life.

03: Defining Success on Your Own Terms

Success means different things to different people. For some, it might mean achieving a high-paying job or becoming famous. For others, it might mean living a simple life surrounded by loved ones. However, regardless of how success is defined, it's important to define it on your own terms.

Why Define Success on Your Own Terms?

Defining success on your own terms is important because it helps you focus on what truly matters to you. It's easy to get caught up in society's definition of success and chase after things that aren't meaningful to you. But when you define success on your own terms, you can focus on achieving goals that align with your values and priorities.

When you define success on your own terms, you're also more likely to feel fulfilled. Pursuing goals that don't align with your values can leave you feeling unfulfilled and empty, even if you achieve them. But when you pursue goals that are meaningful to you, you're more likely to feel a sense of purpose and fulfillment.

03: DEFINING SUCCESS ON YOUR OWN TERMS

Steps to Defining Success on Your Own Terms

Defining success on your own terms is a process that takes time and reflection. Here are some steps you can take to define success on your own terms:

Identify your values: Your values are the things that are most important to you in life. They are the principles that guide your decisions and actions. To define success on your own terms, you need to first identify your values. Take some time to reflect on what matters most to you. Write down a list of your top values.

Reflect on your priorities: Once you've identified your values, reflect on your priorities. What are the things that you prioritize in your life? Is it family, career, personal growth, or something else? Priorities can change over time, so it's important to regularly reflect on them.

Set meaningful goals: Based on your values and priorities, set meaningful goals. These are the goals that align with your values and help you fulfill your priorities. When setting goals, make sure they are specific, measurable, achievable, relevant, and time-bound.

Celebrate progress: Celebrate progress along the way. It's easy to get caught up in achieving the end goal and forget to celebrate the small wins along the way. Celebrating progress can help you stay motivated and feel a sense of accomplishment.

Reevaluate and adjust: Finally, regularly reevaluate and adjust your definition of success. As you grow and evolve, your definition of success may change. It's important to regularly check in with yourself and make sure your goals and priorities are still aligned with your values.

Examples of Defining Success on Your Own Terms

Here are some examples of people who have defined success on their own terms:

Oprah Winfrey: Oprah Winfrey is one of the most successful media personalities in history. However, she defines success on her own terms. For Oprah, success isn't just about making money or becoming famous. It's about using her platform to make a positive impact on the world.

Arianna Huffington: Arianna Huffington is the founder of The Huffington Post. She defines success on her own terms by prioritizing her health and well-being. She has written extensively about the importance of getting enough sleep and taking care of oneself.

Tony Robbins: Tony Robbins is a well-known motivational speaker and author. He defines success on his own terms by focusing on personal growth and helping others achieve their goals.

Conclusion

Defining success on your own terms is an important step in achieving true fulfillment in life. By identifying your values, reflecting on your priorities, setting meaningful goals, celebrating progress, and regularly reevaluating and adjusting your definition of success, you can achieve success on your own terms. Remember, success isn't just about achieving external milestones, it's about living a life that is meaningful and fulfilling to you. When you define success on your own terms, you can create a life that is aligned with your values, priorities, and goals.

It's important to remember that defining success on your own terms is a personal journey. What works for one person may not work for another. It's important to take the time to reflect on what success means to you and create a plan that aligns with your unique values and priorities.

One of the keys to defining success on your own terms is to focus on intrinsic motivation rather than extrinsic motivation. Intrinsic motivation comes from within, such as a sense of purpose, passion, and personal growth. Extrinsic motivation comes from external sources, such as money, fame, and status. While extrinsic motivation can be helpful, it's important not to rely solely on it to define success.

Another important aspect of defining success on your own terms is to stay true to yourself. It can be easy to get caught up in comparing yourself to others or trying to fit into societal expectations of success. But staying true to yourself means being authentic and living a life that is aligned with your unique values and priorities.

Finally, it's important to be flexible and adaptable when defining success on your own terms. Life is full of unexpected twists and turns, and your definition of success may change over time. It's important to regularly reflect on your goals and priorities and adjust them as necessary to stay aligned with your values.

03: DEFINING SUCCESS ON YOUR OWN TERMS

In conclusion, defining success on your own terms is an important step in achieving true fulfillment in life. By identifying your values, reflecting on your priorities, setting meaningful goals, celebrating progress, and regularly reevaluating and adjusting your definition of success, you can create a life that is aligned with your unique values and priorities. Remember, success is a personal journey, and it's important to stay true to yourself and focus on intrinsic motivation.

04: Understanding Purpose and Its Role in Fulfillment

Introduction

Purpose is an essential aspect of human life that brings meaning and fulfillment to our existence. It is the reason why we wake up every morning and strive towards achieving our goals. Purpose is what drives us to be the best version of ourselves and to contribute positively to society.

In this chapter, we will explore the concept of purpose, its importance in our lives, and how we can identify and pursue our purpose to achieve fulfillment.

What is Purpose?

Purpose is the reason why we exist. It is the driving force behind our actions and decisions. Purpose is what gives us direction and helps us to make sense of our lives. Without purpose, life can feel meaningless and empty.

Purpose can take many forms, and it is different for everyone. Some people find their purpose in their careers, while others find it in their families, hobbies, or personal passions. The key is to identify what gives our lives meaning and pursue it with intention and purpose.

The Importance of Purpose

Having a sense of purpose is essential for our overall well-being and happiness. When we have a clear understanding of our purpose, we are more motivated, focused, and resilient in the face of challenges.

Studies have shown that people who have a strong sense of purpose are more likely to live longer, healthier lives. They also experience less stress and anxiety, have better mental health, and are more satisfied with their lives overall.

Additionally, having a sense of purpose helps us to connect with others and contribute to society in meaningful ways. When we are aligned with our purpose, we can make a positive impact on the world around us and leave a lasting legacy.

Identifying Your Purpose

Identifying your purpose can be a challenging and deeply personal process. It requires introspection, self-awareness, and a willingness to explore your passions and values.

Here are some steps you can take to identify your purpose:

Reflect on your values and beliefs

Your purpose is closely tied to your values and beliefs. Take some time to reflect on what is important to you and what you stand for. Ask yourself, what are the causes or issues that resonate with me? What do I care about most deeply?

Explore your passions and interests

Your purpose is often connected to the things that bring you joy and fulfillment. Take some time to explore your passions and interests. What do you enjoy doing in your free time? What are the hobbies or activities that make you feel most alive?

Consider your strengths and talents

Your purpose is also closely tied to your strengths and talents. Consider the things that you are naturally good at and that come easily to you. Ask yourself, how can I use my talents to make a positive impact on the world?

Think about the impact you want to make

04: UNDERSTANDING PURPOSE AND ITS ROLE IN FULFILLMENT

Your purpose is not just about you. It is also about the impact you want to make on the world. Think about the difference you want to make and the legacy you want to leave behind.

Pursuing Your Purpose

Once you have identified your purpose, it is essential to pursue it with intention and purpose. Here are some steps you can take to pursue your purpose:

Set goals that align with your purpose

Your purpose should guide your goals and actions. Set goals that align with your purpose and are in line with your values and beliefs. This will help you stay motivated and focused on what matters most to you.

Take action towards your purpose

Identifying your purpose is just the first step. It is essential to take action towards your purpose every day. This can be as simple as volunteering for a cause you care about, pursuing a new hobby, or making small changes in your daily routine that align with your purpose.

04: UNDERSTANDING PURPOSE AND ITS ROLE IN FULFILLMENT

Surround yourself with supportive people

Having a strong support system is essential when pursuing your purpose. Surround yourself with people who support and encourage you in your journey towards fulfillment. Seek out like-minded individuals who share your values and passions, and who can help you stay motivated and inspired.

Embrace challenges and setbacks

Pursuing your purpose can be challenging, and setbacks are inevitable. Embrace these challenges as opportunities for growth and learning. Remember that setbacks are not failures, but rather opportunities to learn and adapt.

Practice gratitude

Gratitude is a powerful tool for cultivating a sense of purpose and fulfillment. Take time each day to reflect on the things you are grateful for, and how they align with your purpose. This can help you stay motivated and focused on what truly matters in your life.

Conclusion

04: UNDERSTANDING PURPOSE AND ITS ROLE IN FULFILLMENT

In conclusion, purpose is an essential aspect of human life that brings meaning and fulfillment to our existence. It is the reason why we wake up every morning and strive towards achieving our goals. Purpose is what drives us to be the best version of ourselves and to contribute positively to society.

Identifying and pursuing your purpose can be a challenging and deeply personal process. It requires introspection, self-awareness, and a willingness to explore your passions and values. However, the rewards of living a purpose-driven life are immeasurable. When we are aligned with our purpose, we can make a positive impact on the world around us and leave a lasting legacy.

Remember that your purpose is unique to you and may evolve over time. Stay open to new experiences, embrace challenges, and practice gratitude along the way. With perseverance and determination, you can unlock the secrets to lasting happiness, purpose, and success.

05: Identifying Your Values and Beliefs

As human beings, we are all unique and have our own sets of values and beliefs that shape our personalities, behavior, and perspectives. These values and beliefs are often influenced by our upbringing, culture, religion, education, and life experiences. They are the fundamental principles that guide us in our daily lives and help us make decisions, both big and small. Identifying your values and beliefs is a crucial step in achieving true fulfillment in life because they serve as the foundation of your personal growth and development.

So, what exactly are values and beliefs, and how do they differ from each other? Values are the things that we hold dear and are important to us. They are the principles that we live by and the ideals that we strive for. Values can be abstract concepts such as love, honesty, respect, and integrity, or they can be more concrete, such as family, career, health, and wealth. Beliefs, on the other hand, are the ideas and opinions that we hold to be true. They are our convictions about the world, other people, and ourselves. Beliefs can be positive or negative, empowering or limiting, and they can influence our thoughts, emotions, and behaviors.

Identifying your values and beliefs requires a deep level of self-reflection and introspection. It involves examining your thoughts, feelings, and behaviors to determine what really matters to you and what drives you. Here are some steps to help you identify your values and beliefs:

Take time to reflect: Set aside some time to reflect on what is truly important to you. This could be through meditation, journaling, or just quiet contemplation. Ask yourself questions such as: What makes me happy? What are my passions and interests? What are my strengths and weaknesses? What are my goals and aspirations? What do I want to achieve in life?

Identify your core values: Think about the things that you value most in life. These could be qualities such as honesty, kindness, compassion, or they could be specific goals such as financial stability, career success, or personal growth. Write down your top five to ten values.

Explore your beliefs: Think about the beliefs that you hold to be true. Ask yourself questions such as: What do I believe about myself? What do I believe about the world? What do I believe about other people? Are these beliefs empowering or limiting? Write down your beliefs and examine them critically.

Align your values and beliefs: Once you have identified your values and beliefs, examine how they align with each other. Do your beliefs support your values? Are there any conflicts between your values and beliefs? If so, how can you resolve them?

Live your values: Now that you have identified your values and beliefs, it's time to live them. Make a commitment to yourself to live by your values and align your beliefs with them. This means making choices that are in line with your values and beliefs, even if they are difficult or unpopular.

Identifying your values and beliefs is an ongoing process. As you go through life, your values and beliefs may change or evolve. It's important to regularly reflect on them and make adjustments as necessary. When you live in alignment with your values and beliefs, you will experience a greater sense of purpose, happiness, and fulfillment in life.

Here are some additional tips to help you identify and live your values and beliefs:

05: IDENTIFYING YOUR VALUES AND BELIEFS

Surround yourself with like-minded people: Surrounding yourself with people who share your values and beliefs can help reinforce them and provide a sense of community. Seek out friends, family members, or colleagues who share similar values and beliefs as you.

Practice mindfulness: Mindfulness is the practice of being present and aware of your thoughts, emotions, and sensations without judgment. Practicing mindfulness can help you become more aware of your values and beliefs and how they impact your life.

Take action: Identifying your values and beliefs is just the first step. It's important to take action to live by them. This means making choices and taking actions that align with your values and beliefs, even if it's challenging or uncomfortable.

Be open-minded: It's important to be open-minded and flexible when it comes to your values and beliefs. It's okay to adjust or modify them as you learn and grow.

Seek guidance: If you're struggling to identify your values and beliefs or align them with your life, seek guidance from a therapist, coach, or mentor. They can provide valuable insights and support to help you on your journey.

Identifying your values and beliefs is a powerful tool for achieving true fulfillment in life. When you live in alignment with your values and beliefs, you will experience a greater sense of purpose, happiness, and success. Take the time to reflect on your values and beliefs, make a commitment to live by them, and seek support when needed. With dedication and effort, you can unlock the secrets to lasting happiness, purpose, and success.

06: Overcoming Self-Limiting Beliefs

Introduction

Self-limiting beliefs are negative thoughts that we have about ourselves, our abilities, and our potential. These beliefs often stem from past experiences or feedback we have received from others. When we believe these negative thoughts, we limit our potential and prevent ourselves from achieving our goals and dreams. In this chapter, we will explore the various ways in which self-limiting beliefs can hold us back and provide practical strategies for overcoming them.

The Impact of Self-Limiting Beliefs

Self-limiting beliefs can have a profound impact on our lives. They can prevent us from taking risks, pursuing our passions, and achieving our goals. When we believe that we are not capable of achieving something, we are less likely to put in the effort required to make it happen. This can lead to a lack of confidence, self-doubt, and feelings of inadequacy.

Self-limiting beliefs can also limit our career prospects. If we believe that we are not capable of achieving success in our chosen field, we may not put in the effort required to excel. This can lead to missed opportunities and a lack of career progression.

The good news is that self-limiting beliefs can be overcome. By identifying and challenging these beliefs, we can change our mindset and unlock our full potential.

Identifying Self-Limiting Beliefs

The first step in overcoming self-limiting beliefs is to identify them. This can be a challenging process as these beliefs are often deeply ingrained in our subconscious. However, by paying attention to our thoughts and feelings, we can begin to identify patterns of negative thinking.

One way to identify self-limiting beliefs is to write down any negative thoughts or beliefs that come to mind. This can be done in a journal or on a piece of paper. Once you have identified these thoughts, ask yourself the following questions:

– Is this belief true?

– What evidence do I have to support this belief?

– What evidence do I have to contradict this belief?

By challenging your beliefs in this way, you can begin to see them in a more objective light.

Challenging Self-Limiting Beliefs

Once you have identified your self-limiting beliefs, the next step is to challenge them. This can be done by asking yourself the following questions:

– What is the evidence for this belief?

– What is the evidence against this belief?

– What is the worst thing that could happen if this belief is not true?

– What is the best thing that could happen if this belief is not true?

By challenging your beliefs in this way, you can begin to see that they are not necessarily true or accurate.

Replacing Self-Limiting Beliefs with Positive Affirmations

06: OVERCOMING SELF-LIMITING BELIEFS

Once you have challenged your self-limiting beliefs, it is important to replace them with positive affirmations. Positive affirmations are statements that reflect the positive traits and abilities that you possess. By repeating these affirmations to yourself on a regular basis, you can begin to change your mindset and build your self-confidence.

Examples of positive affirmations include:

– I am capable of achieving anything I set my mind to.

– I am worthy of love and respect.

– I have the ability to overcome any obstacle that comes my way.

– I am strong and resilient.

By repeating these affirmations to yourself on a daily basis, you can begin to build your self-confidence and overcome your self-limiting beliefs.

Seeking Support

Finally, it is important to seek support when overcoming self-limiting beliefs. This can be done by talking to friends and family members who can provide encouragement and support. It can also be helpful to seek the advice of a professional therapist who can provide guidance and support as you work to overcome your self-limiting beliefs.

Conclusion

Self-limiting beliefs can hold us back and prevent us from achieving our full potential. However, by identifying, challenging, and replacing these beliefs with positive affirmations, we can overcome them and unlock our true potential. It is important to remember that overcoming self-limiting beliefs is a process and it may take time to fully eliminate these beliefs.

As you work to overcome your self-limiting beliefs, remember to be patient and kind to yourself. It can be challenging to change deeply ingrained thought patterns, but with time and effort, it is possible. By seeking support and practicing self-care, you can overcome your self-limiting beliefs and achieve true fulfillment in life.

In addition to the strategies discussed in this chapter, there are many other techniques that can be used to overcome self-limiting beliefs. These include visualization, meditation, and mindfulness practices. It is important to find the techniques that work best for you and to practice them consistently.

Remember, self-limiting beliefs are not permanent. By taking the time to identify and challenge these beliefs, you can transform your mindset and achieve the success and fulfillment you deserve. You have the power to create the life you want, so don't let self-limiting beliefs hold you back.

07: Cultivating a Growth Mindset

Introduction

Have you ever felt like you're stuck in life? That you've reached a plateau and can't seem to make any progress? If so, you're not alone. Many people struggle with feeling unfulfilled and stuck in their lives, not sure how to move forward. But what if I told you that the key to unlocking lasting happiness, purpose, and success is within your reach? It's all about cultivating a growth mindset.

In this chapter, we'll explore what a growth mindset is, why it's important, and how you can start cultivating one today. By the end of this chapter, you'll have a deeper understanding of yourself and the tools you need to achieve true fulfillment in life.

What is a Growth Mindset?

A growth mindset is the belief that your abilities and intelligence can be developed through hard work, dedication, and persistence. In contrast, a fixed mindset is the belief that your abilities and intelligence are predetermined and unchangeable.

People with a growth mindset see challenges as opportunities for growth and learning. They embrace failure as a natural part of the learning process and view it as an opportunity to improve. They're open to feedback and criticism, and they use it to improve their skills and abilities.

In contrast, people with a fixed mindset see challenges as threats to their abilities and intelligence. They avoid failure at all costs and view it as a sign of weakness or incompetence. They're defensive in the face of feedback and criticism and may even become hostile or dismissive.

Why is a Growth Mindset Important?

A growth mindset is essential for personal growth and development. It allows you to see the potential for growth and improvement in every situation. With a growth mindset, you're not limited by your current abilities or intelligence. You have the power to change and improve through hard work and dedication.

A growth mindset also helps you deal with setbacks and failures in a healthy way. Instead of giving up or feeling defeated, you see failure as an opportunity to learn and grow. This resilience and perseverance are essential for achieving success in any area of life.

How to Cultivate a Growth Mindset

Now that you understand what a growth mindset is and why it's important, let's explore how you can cultivate one.

Embrace Challenges

People with a growth mindset embrace challenges as opportunities for growth and learning. They see them as a chance to push themselves out of their comfort zones and develop new skills and abilities. Instead of avoiding challenges, seek them out. Look for opportunities to stretch yourself and take on new challenges.

Embrace Failure

Failure is a natural part of the learning process. People with a growth mindset embrace failure as an opportunity to learn and improve. Instead of avoiding failure, embrace it. Learn from your mistakes and use them as an opportunity to grow.

Learn from Feedback

People with a growth mindset are open to feedback and criticism. They see it as an opportunity to learn and improve. Instead of becoming defensive, listen to feedback and consider how you can use it to improve your skills and abilities.

Cultivate a Love of Learning

People with a growth mindset are lifelong learners. They're curious and always seeking to learn new things. Cultivate a love of learning by reading, taking courses, and exploring new areas of interest.

Surround Yourself with Positive Role Models

Surround yourself with people who have a growth mindset. Seek out positive role models who embody the traits you want to cultivate in yourself. Spend time with people who inspire and motivate you to grow and develop.

Practice Self-Compassion

Finally, practice self-compassion. People with a growth mindset are kind to themselves and recognize that growth and development take time. Be patient with yourself and celebrate your progress, no matter how small.

Conclusion

Cultivating a growth mindset is essential for achieving true fulfillment in life. It allows you to see challenges as opportunities for growth and learning, and failure as an opportunity to learn and improve. It also helps you develop resilience and perseverance, which are essential for achieving success in any area of life.

To cultivate a growth mindset, you need to embrace challenges, failure, and feedback. You should also cultivate a love of learning, surround yourself with positive role models, and practice self-compassion. By doing so, you'll develop a deep sense of self-awareness and the tools you need to achieve true fulfillment in life.

Remember that cultivating a growth mindset is a lifelong journey. It takes time, dedication, and hard work. But the rewards are immeasurable. With a growth mindset, you'll be able to achieve your goals, overcome obstacles, and live a life of true fulfillment and purpose.

In the end, it all comes down to your mindset. If you believe that you can develop your abilities and intelligence through hard work and dedication, then you'll be able to achieve anything you set your mind to. But if you believe that your abilities and intelligence are predetermined and unchangeable, then you'll be limited by your own self-imposed limitations.

So, embrace a growth mindset and unlock the secrets to lasting happiness, purpose, and success. Remember that you have the power to change and improve, and that every challenge and failure is an opportunity for growth and learning. With a growth mindset, anything is possible, and true fulfillment in life is within your reach.

08: Developing a Positive Attitude

Developing a positive attitude is one of the most important steps towards achieving true fulfillment in life. A positive attitude can help you overcome obstacles, build strong relationships, and achieve your goals. However, developing a positive attitude is not always easy, especially if you are going through a difficult time in your life. In this chapter, we will explore the importance of a positive attitude and provide practical tips for cultivating one.

The Importance of a Positive Attitude

A positive attitude is a state of mind in which you approach life with optimism, hope, and confidence. A positive attitude can have a profound impact on your life in many ways. Here are just a few examples:

Improved Mental Health: A positive attitude can help you manage stress and anxiety, which can improve your mental health. When you approach life with a positive mindset, you are better able to cope with the challenges and setbacks that come your way.

Enhanced Relationships: A positive attitude can also improve your relationships with others. When you have a positive outlook on life, you are more likely to be kind, compassionate, and understanding towards others. This can lead to stronger, more meaningful relationships.

Increased Success: A positive attitude can also help you achieve your goals. When you believe in yourself and approach challenges with a can-do attitude, you are more likely to succeed. A positive attitude can also help you stay motivated and persistent in the face of obstacles.

Tips for Cultivating a Positive Attitude

Now that we understand the importance of a positive attitude, let's explore some practical tips for cultivating one.

Practice Gratitude: One of the most effective ways to cultivate a positive attitude is to practice gratitude. Take a few minutes each day to reflect on the things in your life that you are grateful for. This can include anything from your health and family to your job and hobbies.

Focus on the Positive: Another way to cultivate a positive attitude is to focus on the positive aspects of your life. Instead of dwelling on the negative, try to find the silver lining in every situation. For example, if you are stuck in traffic, use the time to listen to your favorite podcast or enjoy the scenery.

Surround Yourself with Positive People: Your environment can have a big impact on your attitude. Surround yourself with positive people who uplift and encourage you. Avoid negative people who bring you down and drain your energy.

Practice Self-Care: Taking care of yourself is essential for cultivating a positive attitude. Make time for activities that bring you joy, such as exercise, reading, or spending time with loved ones. Remember to also prioritize self-care activities such as getting enough sleep, eating well, and practicing mindfulness.

Challenge Negative Thoughts: Negative self-talk can be a major barrier to developing a positive attitude. When you notice negative thoughts creeping in, challenge them with positive affirmations. For example, if you find yourself thinking, "I'm not good enough," counteract that thought with a positive affirmation such as, "I am capable and worthy of success."

Set Realistic Goals: Setting realistic goals can also help you develop a positive attitude. When you set goals that are achievable, you are more likely to experience success and feel motivated to continue working towards your goals.

Learn from Failure: Failure is a natural part of life, and it can be difficult to stay positive when things don't go as planned. However, learning from failure can be a powerful tool for cultivating a positive attitude. Instead of beating yourself up over a setback, try to identify what you can learn from the experience and how you can use that knowledge to improve in the future.

In Conclusion

Developing a positive attitude is essential for achieving true fulfillment in life. A positive attitude can help you overcome obstacles, build strong relationships, and achieve your goals. By practicing gratitude, focusing on the positive, surrounding yourself with positive people, practicing self-care, challenging negative thoughts, setting realistic goals, and learning from failure, you can cultivate a positive attitude that will serve you well in all areas of your life.

Remember that developing a positive attitude is a journey, not a destination. It takes time and effort to change your mindset, but the rewards are well worth it. Don't be discouraged if you experience setbacks along the way. Keep practicing these tips and you will gradually begin to see a positive change in your attitude and overall outlook on life.

It's also important to note that cultivating a positive attitude does not mean ignoring or suppressing negative emotions. It's important to acknowledge and process negative emotions in a healthy way. However, by focusing on the positive and adopting a more optimistic mindset, you can navigate difficult situations with greater resilience and come out the other side stronger than ever.

In conclusion, developing a positive attitude is a crucial step towards achieving true fulfillment in life. By practicing gratitude, focusing on the positive, surrounding yourself with positive people, practicing self-care, challenging negative thoughts, setting realistic goals, and learning from failure, you can cultivate a positive attitude that will serve you well in all areas of your life. Keep at it, and remember that the journey towards a positive attitude is a lifelong one.

09: Building Strong Relationships

One of the most important aspects of leading a fulfilling life is having strong relationships with those around us. Whether it's with our family, friends, or significant other, relationships are crucial to our happiness and well-being. They provide us with support, love, and a sense of belonging. In this chapter, we'll discuss the key components of building strong relationships and how they can contribute to our overall sense of fulfillment.

Communication

Effective communication is the foundation of any strong relationship. It's important to communicate openly and honestly with those we care about, expressing our thoughts, feelings, and needs in a respectful manner. This not only helps us to feel heard and understood, but it also allows us to understand the other person's perspective. Without good communication, misunderstandings can arise and problems can fester, leading to resentment and distance in the relationship.

Trust

Trust is a crucial component of any strong relationship. It's important to trust that the other person has our best interests at heart and will act in accordance with our shared values. Trust is built over time, through consistent actions that demonstrate reliability, honesty, and integrity. When trust is broken, it can be difficult to repair, so it's important to nurture and protect it.

Respect

Respect is another essential component of strong relationships. It's important to respect each other's boundaries, opinions, and values, even if they differ from our own. This requires empathy and the ability to see things from another person's perspective. When we show respect to others, we demonstrate that we value and care about them, which strengthens our connection.

Shared experiences

Shared experiences can help to deepen our relationships and create lasting memories. Whether it's traveling together, trying new activities, or simply spending quality time together, shared experiences can help to strengthen our bond and create a sense of closeness. When we share experiences with others, we're able to connect on a deeper level and build a stronger foundation for our relationship.

Forgiveness

No relationship is perfect, and conflicts are bound to arise from time to time. It's important to be willing to forgive and move forward when misunderstandings or disagreements occur. Forgiveness requires empathy, understanding, and the ability to let go of grudges and resentments. When we're able to forgive and move forward, we demonstrate our commitment to the relationship and our willingness to work through challenges together.

Quality time

Spending quality time together is essential for building strong relationships. Whether it's a weekly date night with a significant other, a regular family dinner, or a weekend getaway with friends, setting aside time to connect and bond is important for nurturing our relationships. When we prioritize quality time, we demonstrate that we value and prioritize our relationships.

Authenticity

Finally, it's important to be authentic and true to ourselves in our relationships. When we're able to be our true selves, we create space for others to do the same, which can deepen our connection and strengthen our relationship. Authenticity requires vulnerability and the willingness to be seen and accepted for who we truly are. When we're able to be authentic with others, we create a sense of trust and safety in the relationship, which can help us to feel more fulfilled and connected.

In summary, building strong relationships requires effective communication, trust, respect, shared experiences, forgiveness, quality time, and authenticity. When we prioritize these key components, we can create deeper connections with those around us and experience a greater sense of fulfillment in our lives.

10: Communicating Effectively

Communication is one of the most important skills anyone can possess. In order to achieve true fulfillment in life, it is imperative that we learn how to communicate effectively. Communication is not only about what we say, but also how we say it, and the message we convey to others. In this chapter, we will explore the different elements of effective communication and how we can use them to improve our relationships, our work, and our overall sense of purpose and fulfillment.

Understanding Communication

Communication is the process of exchanging information, ideas, and emotions between two or more people. It can take many forms, including verbal, nonverbal, written, and visual. Effective communication involves more than just speaking and listening, it requires empathy, active listening, and the ability to convey ideas clearly and effectively.

One of the most important aspects of effective communication is understanding your audience. Whether you are communicating with a friend, a coworker, or a large group of people, it is essential to tailor your message to their needs and expectations. This means taking into account factors like their knowledge, interests, beliefs, and emotions.

Another key element of effective communication is the ability to read and interpret nonverbal cues. This includes facial expressions, body language, tone of voice, and other subtle cues that can convey important information about a person's thoughts and feelings. Learning to read these cues can help us better understand the people we are communicating with and respond appropriately.

Types of Communication

There are many different types of communication, each with its own strengths and weaknesses. Some of the most common types of communication include:

Verbal Communication: This includes spoken words and can take the form of conversations, speeches, or presentations. Verbal communication is often the most direct and immediate form of communication, but it can also be subject to misunderstandings and misinterpretations.

Nonverbal Communication: This includes body language, facial expressions, and other nonverbal cues that convey information without the use of words. Nonverbal communication can be more subtle and nuanced than verbal communication, but it can also be subject to misinterpretation and cultural differences.

Written Communication: This includes written words and can take the form of emails, letters, reports, or other forms of written communication. Written communication is often more formal and structured than verbal communication, but it can also be less personal and immediate.

Visual Communication: This includes images, graphics, and other visual aids that can be used to convey information. Visual communication can be highly effective in conveying complex ideas and concepts, but it can also be subject to misinterpretation and cultural differences.

Effective Communication Skills

In order to communicate effectively, it is important to develop a range of skills and strategies that can help you convey your message clearly and effectively. Some of the most important skills include:

Active Listening: This involves paying close attention to the person you are communicating with and actively seeking to understand their perspective. Active listening requires focus, empathy, and the ability to ask open-ended questions to clarify your understanding.

Empathy: This involves putting yourself in the other person's shoes and trying to understand their thoughts, feelings, and motivations. Empathy can help you better understand the people you are communicating with and respond in a more compassionate and effective way.

Clarity: This involves using clear and concise language to convey your message. It is important to avoid jargon, technical terms, and other language that may be unfamiliar or confusing to your audience.

Nonverbal Communication: This involves using body language, facial expressions, and other nonverbal cues to convey your message. Nonverbal communication can help reinforce your message and convey important information about your thoughts and feelings.

Feedback: This involves seeking and giving feedback to improve communication. It is important to be open to feedback and willing to make changes to improve your communication skills.

Barriers

Despite our best efforts, communication can still be subject to a range of barriers that can impede our ability to convey our message effectively. Some of the most common barriers to communication include:

Language: Language barriers can arise when people speak different languages or have different levels of proficiency in a shared language. This can make it difficult to understand each other and convey important information.

Culture: Cultural barriers can arise when people have different cultural norms, values, and beliefs. This can affect everything from nonverbal communication to the way people interpret and respond to messages.

Technology: Technology can be a double-edged sword when it comes to communication. While it can facilitate communication across great distances and allow for instant messaging, video conferencing, and other forms of communication, it can also be subject to glitches, delays, and other technical difficulties that can impede effective communication.

Emotions: Strong emotions can interfere with effective communication by clouding our judgment and making it difficult to convey our message clearly and objectively.

Misunderstandings: Misunderstandings can arise when people have different interpretations of the same message. This can occur due to factors like language barriers, cultural differences, and differences in knowledge and experience.

Overcoming these barriers requires a combination of self-awareness, empathy, and effective communication strategies. It is important to be aware of these barriers and take steps to address them proactively, whether that means learning a new language, adapting to a new culture, or using technology effectively.

Tips for Effective Communication

Here are some tips to help you communicate more effectively:

Be Clear and Concise: Use clear and concise language to convey your message. Avoid jargon, technical terms, and other language that may be unfamiliar or confusing to your audience.

Listen Actively: Pay close attention to the person you are communicating with and actively seek to understand their perspective. Ask open-ended questions to clarify your understanding.

Use Nonverbal Cues: Use body language, facial expressions, and other nonverbal cues to convey your message. This can help reinforce your message and convey important information about your thoughts and feelings.

Show Empathy: Put yourself in the other person's shoes and try to understand their thoughts, feelings, and motivations. Respond in a compassionate and effective way.

Use Feedback: Seek and give feedback to improve communication. Be open to feedback and willing to make changes to improve your communication skills.

Adapt to Your Audience: Tailor your message to your audience's needs and expectations. Take into account factors like their knowledge, interests, beliefs, and emotions.

Conclusion

Effective communication is a critical skill that can help us achieve true fulfillment in life. By understanding the different elements of effective communication and developing a range of skills and strategies, we can improve our relationships, our work, and our overall sense of purpose and fulfillment. Remember to listen actively, show empathy, use nonverbal cues, and seek feedback to improve your communication skills. With practice and dedication, anyone can become a more effective communicator and achieve true fulfillment in life.

11: Practicing Empathy and Compassion

As human beings, we all have the capacity for empathy and compassion. These traits allow us to understand and share the feelings of others and to be kind and caring towards them. However, in our fast-paced and often self-centered world, empathy and compassion can sometimes take a backseat to our own concerns and priorities.

But if we want to live a truly fulfilling life, empathy and compassion are essential. Not only do they allow us to connect with others on a deeper level, but they also help us to feel more fulfilled and purposeful in our own lives.

In this chapter, we'll explore the importance of empathy and compassion, how to practice them in our daily lives, and how they can help us achieve true fulfillment.

The Importance of Empathy and Compassion

Empathy and compassion are often used interchangeably, but they are actually two distinct but related traits. Empathy refers to our ability to understand and share the feelings of others, while compassion is the desire to alleviate the suffering of others.

Both empathy and compassion are crucial for building strong and meaningful relationships with others. When we are empathetic, we are able to truly understand and appreciate the perspectives and experiences of those around us. This can help us to communicate more effectively, resolve conflicts more easily, and build deeper connections with others.

Compassion, on the other hand, allows us to show kindness and care towards others. When we feel compassion for someone, we are motivated to help them in whatever way we can, whether it's through simple acts of kindness or more substantial efforts to alleviate their suffering.

But empathy and compassion aren't just important for our relationships with others. They also play a crucial role in our own sense of fulfillment and purpose in life.

When we practice empathy and compassion, we are able to see beyond our own individual concerns and connect with something larger than ourselves. We become part of a larger community of people who are all working to make the world a better place, and we feel a sense of purpose and meaning

11: PRACTICING EMPATHY AND COMPASSION

in our lives.

How to Practice Empathy and Compassion

While empathy and compassion are natural human traits, they are also skills that can be developed and strengthened through practice. Here are some strategies for cultivating empathy and compassion in your daily life:

Listen actively - When you are talking to someone, make a conscious effort to really listen to what they are saying. Put aside your own thoughts and concerns for a moment and focus on understanding their perspective.

Put yourself in their shoes - Try to imagine what it would feel like to be in the other person's situation. How would you feel? What would your concerns be? This can help you to better understand and empathize with their experience.

Practice kindness - Look for opportunities to be kind and caring towards others. This could be as simple as offering a kind word or gesture, or it could involve more substantial efforts to help alleviate their suffering.

Volunteer - Find ways to give back to your community by

volunteering your time or resources. This can help you to connect with others and to feel a sense of purpose and fulfillment in your life.

Practice self-compassion - Remember that empathy and compassion also apply to yourself. Be kind and caring towards yourself, and don't be too hard on yourself when things don't go as planned.

The Benefits of Practicing Empathy and Compassion

There are many benefits to practicing empathy and compassion in your daily life. Here are just a few:

Improved relationships - When you are more empathetic and compassionate towards others, you are able to build stronger and more meaningful relationships with them.

Increased happiness - Helping others and making a positive difference in the world can be incredibly fulfilling and can bring a great deal of happiness and joy into your life.

Reduced stress - When you are focused on the needs and concerns of others, you are less likely to become overly focused on your own worries and concerns, which can help to reduce stress and anxiety.

Increased resilience - Practicing empathy and compassion can help to build resilience and strength in the face of adversity. By focusing on the needs of others, you are able to see beyond your own challenges and can find the strength to overcome them.

Improved physical health - Research has shown that practicing empathy and compassion can have a positive impact on physical health, including reducing inflammation and improving immune function.

In short, practicing empathy and compassion is not only good for those around us, but it is also good for our own well-being and fulfillment in life.

Conclusion

Empathy and compassion are essential traits for living a fulfilling and purposeful life. By taking the time to understand and care for the needs and concerns of others, we are able to build strong relationships, find meaning and purpose in our lives, and make a positive difference in the world.

11: PRACTICING EMPATHY AND COMPASSION

While empathy and compassion may come naturally to some, they are also skills that can be developed and strengthened through practice. By listening actively, putting ourselves in the shoes of others, practicing kindness, volunteering, and practicing self-compassion, we can cultivate these traits and enjoy the many benefits they bring.

So if you want to unlock the secrets to lasting happiness, purpose, and success, start by practicing empathy and compassion in your daily life. It may take effort and practice, but the rewards are well worth it.

12: Developing Emotional Intelligence

Introduction

Emotional intelligence is a crucial component in achieving fulfillment in life. It is the ability to recognize and manage our own emotions, as well as understanding and responding appropriately to the emotions of others. In this chapter, we will discuss the importance of developing emotional intelligence and provide practical steps for enhancing this skill.

Understanding Emotional Intelligence

Emotional intelligence is the ability to perceive and understand emotions, to use emotions to facilitate thought, to manage emotions effectively, and to regulate emotions in oneself and others. It involves four key areas: self-awareness, self-management, social awareness, and relationship management.

Self-awareness is the ability to recognize and understand our own emotions, thoughts, and behaviors. This includes being aware of our strengths and weaknesses, our values, and our goals. It also involves being mindful of our emotional triggers and how we react to them.

Self-management is the ability to control our own emotions and behavior. It involves being able to regulate our emotions in a healthy way and to respond appropriately to different situations. This includes managing stress, controlling impulses, and being adaptable in different situations.

Social awareness is the ability to understand and empathize with the emotions of others. This involves being able to read social cues and to recognize and respond appropriately to the emotions of others. It also involves being able to communicate effectively and to build strong relationships with others.

Relationship management is the ability to use emotional intelligence to build and maintain healthy relationships. This involves being able to communicate effectively, to resolve conflicts in a positive way, and to build trust and respect with others.

Why Emotional Intelligence is Important

Emotional intelligence is important for many reasons. It helps us to understand and manage our own emotions, which can lead to better mental health and well-being. It also helps us to understand and empathize with the emotions of others, which can lead to better relationships and more effective communication.

Emotional intelligence is also important for success in the workplace. Studies have shown that people with higher emotional intelligence are more successful in their careers, have better job satisfaction, and are more likely to be promoted. This is because emotional intelligence is essential for effective leadership, communication, and teamwork.

Finally, emotional intelligence is important for achieving fulfillment in life. When we are able to understand and manage our own emotions, we are more likely to experience positive emotions like joy and contentment. When we are able to understand and empathize with the emotions of others, we are more likely to experience meaningful connections and a sense of purpose.

How to Develop Emotional Intelligence

Developing emotional intelligence is a lifelong process, but there are several practical steps you can take to enhance this skill.

12: DEVELOPING EMOTIONAL INTELLIGENCE

Practice self-awareness: Take time to reflect on your own emotions, thoughts, and behaviors. Pay attention to your emotional triggers and how you react to them. This can help you to better understand your own emotions and to manage them more effectively.

Manage stress: Stress can have a negative impact on emotional intelligence. Take steps to manage stress in a healthy way, such as exercise, meditation, or spending time in nature. This can help you to regulate your emotions and to respond more effectively to different situations.

Practice empathy: Empathy is the ability to understand and share the feelings of others. Practice empathy by listening actively, putting yourself in someone else's shoes, and responding in a supportive and understanding way.

Build positive relationships: Relationships are essential for emotional intelligence. Build positive relationships with others by communicating effectively, showing respect and kindness, and resolving conflicts in a positive way.

Seek feedback: Ask others for feedback on your emotional intelligence. This can help you to identify areas for improvement and to develop strategies for enhancing this skill.

Conclusion

Developing emotional intelligence is essential for achieving fulfillment in life. It involves understanding and managing our own emotions, as well as understanding and responding appropriately to the emotions of others. It is a lifelong process, but with practice and dedication, we can enhance our emotional intelligence and experience greater happiness, purpose, and success in life.

In addition to the practical steps mentioned above, it is important to cultivate a growth mindset. This means believing that our abilities and intelligence can be developed through hard work and dedication. By adopting a growth mindset, we are more likely to embrace challenges and setbacks as opportunities for growth and learning, which can help us to develop greater emotional intelligence.

Another important aspect of developing emotional intelligence is self-compassion. This involves treating ourselves with kindness and understanding, especially in times of difficulty or failure. When we practice self-compassion, we are more likely to be resilient in the face of adversity and to bounce back from setbacks.

It is also important to recognize that emotional intelligence is not a fixed trait. While some people may be naturally more emotionally intelligent than others, everyone has the potential to develop this skill. By committing to ongoing personal growth and development, we can continue to enhance our emotional intelligence throughout our lives.

Finally, it is important to remember that emotional intelligence is not a panacea for all of life's challenges. While it can certainly help us to navigate difficult emotions and relationships, it is not a substitute for professional mental health support when needed. If you are struggling with your emotional well-being, consider seeking the help of a qualified mental health professional.

In conclusion, developing emotional intelligence is a key component of achieving fulfillment in life. By practicing self-awareness, managing stress, practicing empathy, building positive relationships, seeking feedback, cultivating a growth mindset, practicing self-compassion, and committing to ongoing personal growth and development, we can enhance our emotional intelligence and experience greater happiness, purpose, and success in life.

13: Overcoming Fear and Anxiety

Fear and anxiety are two of the most common emotions that people experience in their lives. While both emotions serve as important warning signals, they can also cause significant distress and hinder a person's ability to achieve their goals and dreams. In this chapter, we will explore the causes and effects of fear and anxiety and provide practical tips and techniques for overcoming these emotions and achieving true fulfillment in life.

Understanding Fear and Anxiety

Fear and anxiety are two distinct emotions, although they are often used interchangeably. Fear is an emotional response to an immediate threat or danger, while anxiety is a response to a perceived threat or uncertainty about the future. Fear is a necessary and natural response that has evolved to keep us safe from harm, while anxiety can be both helpful and harmful depending on the situation.

Both fear and anxiety activate the body's stress response, triggering the release of stress hormones such as cortisol and adrenaline. These hormones increase heart rate, blood pressure, and respiration, preparing the body for a fight-or-flight response. In small doses, this response can be helpful in boosting alertness and focus, but prolonged exposure to stress hormones can have harmful effects on physical and mental health.

Causes of Fear and Anxiety

Fear and anxiety can be caused by a variety of factors, including past experiences, genetic predisposition, and current circumstances. Traumatic experiences, such as abuse or a natural disaster, can leave a lasting impact on a person's emotional and mental well-being, leading to fear and anxiety in future situations that remind them of the trauma.

Genetics also play a role in the development of fear and anxiety. Research has shown that some people may be more prone to anxiety due to genetic factors that influence brain chemistry and function.

Current circumstances, such as financial difficulties, relationship problems, or health issues, can also trigger fear and anxiety. The uncertainty and unpredictability of these situations can make it difficult for people to feel in control of their lives, leading to feelings of fear and anxiety.

Effects of Fear and Anxiety

13: OVERCOMING FEAR AND ANXIETY

The effects of fear and anxiety can be both physical and mental. In the short term, fear and anxiety can cause symptoms such as sweating, trembling, and a rapid heartbeat. These physical symptoms can be uncomfortable and distressing, leading to further anxiety and fear.

Over time, fear and anxiety can have more serious effects on a person's physical and mental health. Chronic stress can increase the risk of heart disease, stroke, and other health problems. Anxiety can also lead to depression, social isolation, and substance abuse, further exacerbating the negative effects on a person's life.

Tips for Overcoming Fear and Anxiety

While fear and anxiety can be challenging to overcome, there are many practical tips and techniques that can help. Here are some strategies for managing fear and anxiety and achieving true fulfillment in life:

Identify the source of your fear and anxiety.

The first step in overcoming fear and anxiety is to identify the source of your emotions. Is there a particular situation or event that is triggering your fear and anxiety? Once you have identified the source of your emotions, you can begin to develop strategies for managing them.

Practice mindfulness and relaxation techniques.

Mindfulness and relaxation techniques, such as deep breathing, meditation, and yoga, can be effective in reducing stress and anxiety. By focusing on the present moment and letting go of distracting thoughts, you can calm your mind and reduce feelings of fear and anxiety.

Challenge negative thoughts and beliefs.

Negative thoughts and beliefs can fuel fear and anxiety, making it difficult to break free from these emotions. By challenging these thoughts and replacing them with more positive and realistic ones, you can reduce the impact of fear and anxiety on your life.

Seek support from others.

Talking to friends, family members, or a mental health professional can be helpful in managing fear and anxiety. Sharing your emotions and experiences with others can provide a sense of connection and support, and can help you to feel less alone in your struggles.

Practice self-care.

Taking care of your physical, emotional, and mental well-being is essential for managing fear and anxiety. This includes getting enough sleep, eating a healthy diet, exercising regularly, and engaging in activities that bring you joy and fulfillment.

Set achievable goals.

Setting achievable goals can help you to feel more in control of your life and reduce feelings of uncertainty and anxiety. Start with small goals that you know you can accomplish, and gradually work your way up to more challenging goals.

Challenge yourself to face your fears.

While it can be tempting to avoid situations that trigger fear and anxiety, confronting these situations can help you to overcome these emotions. Start by facing small fears and gradually work your way up to more challenging ones.

Practice gratitude.

13: OVERCOMING FEAR AND ANXIETY

Practicing gratitude and focusing on the positive aspects of your life can help to counteract feelings of fear and anxiety. Take time each day to reflect on what you are thankful for and what is going well in your life.

Conclusion

Fear and anxiety are common emotions that can have significant impacts on a person's life. While these emotions can be challenging to overcome, there are many practical tips and techniques that can help. By identifying the source of your emotions, practicing mindfulness and relaxation techniques, challenging negative thoughts, seeking support from others, practicing self-care, setting achievable goals, facing your fears, and practicing gratitude, you can overcome fear and anxiety and achieve true fulfillment in life.

14: Managing Stress and Pressure

Stress and pressure are two of the most common challenges people face in their daily lives. Whether it is related to work, relationships, or personal issues, stress and pressure can be overwhelming and cause a great deal of physical and emotional distress. However, managing stress and pressure is essential to maintaining good mental and physical health, achieving your goals, and living a fulfilling life.

In this chapter, we will explore the causes of stress and pressure, the negative effects they can have on our well-being, and most importantly, some effective strategies for managing them.

Understanding Stress and Pressure

Stress is a natural response to any demand or challenge that requires our attention, energy, or resources. It can be caused by a variety of factors, including work, relationships, financial problems, health issues, or major life events such as divorce or the death of a loved one. When we encounter a stressful situation, our bodies release hormones such as adrenaline and cortisol, which trigger the "fight or flight" response. This response helps us to respond quickly and effectively to danger, but it can also cause physical symptoms such as increased heart rate, rapid breathing, and muscle tension.

Pressure, on the other hand, is often related to expectations and the perceived consequences of failure. For example, you may feel pressure to meet a deadline at work or to perform well on an exam. The pressure can be internal or external, and it can be influenced by factors such as our own goals and values, the expectations of others, and the consequences of failure or success.

The Negative Effects of Stress and Pressure

While some stress and pressure can be beneficial, chronic or excessive stress and pressure can have a negative impact on our mental and physical health. Some common effects of stress and pressure include:

Anxiety and Depression: Chronic stress can lead to anxiety and depression, which can have a significant impact on our quality of life.

Physical Health Problems: Chronic stress can also lead to physical health problems such as high blood pressure, heart disease, and digestive problems.

Poor Sleep: Stress and pressure can make it difficult to fall asleep or stay asleep, leading to fatigue and other health problems.

Decreased Productivity: High levels of stress and pressure can decrease productivity, making it difficult to achieve our goals and fulfill our responsibilities.

Effective Strategies for Managing Stress and Pressure

Fortunately, there are many effective strategies for managing stress and pressure. Some of these strategies include:

Exercise: Exercise is one of the most effective ways to manage stress and pressure. Regular exercise can help to reduce anxiety and depression, improve sleep quality, and boost energy levels.

Mindfulness: Mindfulness is a technique that involves focusing on the present moment without judgment. It can help to reduce stress and anxiety and improve overall well-being.

Time Management: Effective time management can help to reduce stress and pressure by ensuring that we have enough time to complete our tasks and meet our deadlines.

Social Support: Having a strong support system can help to reduce stress and pressure by providing emotional support and practical assistance when needed.

Relaxation Techniques: Relaxation techniques such as deep breathing, meditation, and yoga can help to reduce stress and anxiety and improve overall well-being.

Self-Care: Taking care of ourselves is essential for managing stress and pressure. This can involve activities such as getting enough sleep, eating a healthy diet, and engaging in hobbies or activities that bring us joy and relaxation.

Conclusion

Managing stress and pressure is essential for maintaining good mental and physical health, achieving our goals, and living a fulfilling life. By understanding the causes and effects of stress and pressure, and by using effective strategies for managing them, we can reduce the negative impact they have on our well-being and achieve true fulfillment in life. Remember to prioritize self-care and seek support from friends, family, or mental health professionals when needed. With time and practice, we can learn to manage stress and pressure in a healthy and effective way.

In addition to the strategies mentioned above, it's important to also identify and address any underlying causes of stress and pressure. This may involve making changes to our lifestyle, such as reducing our workload, setting boundaries with others, or seeking therapy to work through personal issues.

It's important to note that managing stress and pressure is not a one-time fix, but rather an ongoing process. We may encounter new challenges and sources of stress throughout our lives, and it's important to continue using effective strategies to manage them as they arise.

Ultimately, the key to managing stress and pressure is to prioritize our well-being and take proactive steps to care for ourselves. By doing so, we can achieve true fulfillment and live a happier, healthier, and more purposeful life.

15: Nurturing Your Mental Health

Introduction

In today's fast-paced world, it's easy to become over-whelmed, stressed, and anxious. With so many demands on our time and energy, it's essential to take care of our mental health. Nurturing your mental health is not only important for your well-being but also for your success and happiness in life. In this chapter, we will discuss some practical tips and strategies for taking care of your mental health and achieving true fulfillment in life.

Understanding Mental Health

Before we dive into the practical tips, it's important to understand what mental health is and why it's essential to our overall well-being. Mental health refers to our emotional, psychological, and social well-being. It affects how we think, feel, and behave, and it can impact our ability to cope with stress, interact with others, and make important decisions. Good mental health is vital for a happy, healthy, and fulfilling life.

Common Mental Health Issues

15: NURTURING YOUR MENTAL HEALTH

Mental health issues are more common than we may realize. Some of the most common mental health issues include depression, anxiety, bipolar disorder, post-traumatic stress disorder (PTSD), and obsessive-compulsive disorder (OCD). These conditions can have a significant impact on our daily lives, affecting our relationships, work, and overall quality of life. It's essential to seek professional help if you suspect you may be experiencing a mental health issue.

Tips for Nurturing Your Mental Health

Now that we have a better understanding of mental health let's discuss some practical tips for nurturing your mental health.

Practice Gratitude

One of the simplest and most effective ways to nurture your mental health is to practice gratitude. Taking the time to acknowledge and appreciate the good things in your life can help shift your focus away from negativity and stress. Start by writing down three things you're grateful for each day, no matter how small they may seem. This simple practice can have a profound impact on your mental health and overall well-being.

15: NURTURING YOUR MENTAL HEALTH

Exercise Regularly

Regular exercise is not only great for your physical health but also for your mental health. Exercise has been shown to reduce symptoms of depression, anxiety, and stress, and can even improve cognitive function. Make it a priority to get at least 30 minutes of moderate exercise most days of the week. You don't have to run a marathon to reap the benefits of exercise, either. Walking, yoga, and even gardening can all be great forms of exercise.

Connect with Others

Human beings are social creatures, and it's essential to connect with others to nurture our mental health. Make time for your friends and family, and cultivate new relationships through community groups, volunteering, or other activities. Having a support system can help you through difficult times and provide a sense of purpose and belonging.

Practice Mindfulness

Mindfulness is the practice of being fully present in the moment and non-judgmentally observing your thoughts, feelings, and surroundings. Practicing mindfulness can help reduce stress, anxiety, and depression, and improve overall well-being. Try incorporating mindfulness into your daily routine by setting aside a few minutes each day to practice deep breathing or meditation.

Set Realistic Goals

Having goals and working towards them can provide a sense of purpose and fulfillment. However, it's essential to set realistic goals that are achievable and align with your values. Unrealistic goals can lead to feelings of failure and disappointment, which can negatively impact your mental health. Break down larger goals into smaller, more manageable steps, and celebrate your progress along the way.

Prioritize Self-Care

Self-care is essential for nurturing your mental health. Make it a priority to engage in activities that make you feel good, such as taking a bath, reading a book, or practicing a hobby. Avoid overcommitting yourself and saying yes to things that drain your energy and make you feel overwhelmed. Setting boundaries and prioritizing self-care can help you recharge and maintain good mental health.

15: NURTURING YOUR MENTAL HEALTH

Seek Professional Help

If you're experiencing symptoms of a mental health issue, it's essential to seek professional help. Talk to your doctor or a mental health professional, who can provide a diagnosis and develop a treatment plan tailored to your needs. There is no shame in seeking help, and doing so can lead to improved mental health and overall well-being.

Practice Self-Compassion

Finally, it's essential to practice self-compassion. Treat yourself with kindness, understanding, and forgiveness, just as you would a close friend. Recognize that you're human and make mistakes, and don't beat yourself up for them. Practicing self-compassion can improve your self-esteem and lead to a more positive outlook on life.

Conclusion

Nurturing your mental health is essential for achieving true fulfillment in life. By practicing gratitude, exercising regularly, connecting with others, practicing mindfulness, setting realistic goals, prioritizing self-care, seeking professional help, and practicing self-compassion, you can take steps towards improving your mental health and overall well-being. Remember, good mental health is a journey, not a destination, and it's okay to ask for help along the way.

16: Finding Meaning in Your Work

The average person spends about one-third of their life at work. That's a lot of time to spend doing something that doesn't bring you fulfillment and purpose. If you're feeling unfulfilled or unsatisfied with your job, you're not alone. In fact, studies show that up to 70% of people feel disengaged at work.

But what if you could find meaning in your work? What if your job wasn't just a way to pay the bills, but a way to contribute to something bigger than yourself? What if you could wake up every day excited to go to work, knowing that you were making a difference in the world?

In this chapter, we'll explore the concept of finding meaning in your work. We'll look at the benefits of having a sense of purpose in your job, and we'll provide practical steps you can take to find meaning and fulfillment in your work.

Why Finding Meaning in Your Work Matters

There are many benefits to finding meaning in your work. Here are just a few:

16: FINDING MEANING IN YOUR WORK

Increased motivation and engagement: When you feel like your work has meaning, you're more likely to be motivated and engaged in your job. You'll be more focused, productive, and passionate about what you do.

Greater sense of fulfillment: Finding meaning in your work can give you a greater sense of fulfillment and purpose. You'll feel like you're contributing to something bigger than yourself and making a difference in the world.

Improved mental health: Studies have shown that people who find meaning in their work are less likely to suffer from depression and anxiety. Having a sense of purpose can give you a greater sense of control over your life and reduce feelings of helplessness.

Better relationships: When you're passionate about your work and feel like you're making a difference, you're more likely to have positive relationships with your colleagues and clients. You'll be more approachable, enthusiastic, and helpful.

How to Find Meaning in Your Work

So how can you find meaning in your work? Here are some

practical steps you can take:

Reflect on your values: Think about what's important to you in life. What are your core values? How can you align your work with those values? For example, if you value creativity, you might look for ways to incorporate more creative projects into your job.

Identify your strengths: What are you good at? What skills do you bring to the table? How can you use those strengths in your work? For example, if you're a great communicator, you might look for opportunities to lead meetings or presentations.

Find purpose in your tasks: Even if your job isn't your dream career, there are likely tasks within your job that you find meaningful. Look for ways to connect those tasks to a greater purpose. For example, if you're a customer service representative, you might find purpose in helping people solve problems and have a positive experience.

Seek out opportunities for growth: Feeling stagnant in your job can lead to a lack of fulfillment. Look for ways to grow and develop within your job. Take on new responsibilities, learn new skills, and seek out feedback from your colleagues.

Connect with your colleagues: Building positive relationships with your colleagues can give you a greater sense of purpose and belonging in your job. Take time to get to know your colleagues on a personal level and look for ways to collaborate and support one another.

Give back: Look for opportunities to give back to your community or to support causes that are important to you. Many companies offer volunteer opportunities or charitable giving programs. Giving back can give you a sense of purpose outside of your job and help you feel more connected to your community.

Consider a career change: If you've tried all of the above and still can't find meaning in your job, it may be time to consider a career change. This can be a daunting prospect, but it's important to remember that it's never too late to pursue a career that aligns with your values and passions.

Here are some steps you can take to explore a career change:

Identify your passions: What do you love to do? What activities or hobbies bring you joy? Reflect on your interests and passions to identify potential career paths that align with those passions.

Research potential careers: Once you've identified some potential career paths, research them to learn more about the skills and qualifications required, salary ranges, and job outlook. This can help you determine if a particular career is a good fit for you.

Talk to people in the field: Reach out to people who work in the field you're interested in to learn more about their experiences. Ask about the challenges and rewards of their job, and what it takes to be successful in that field.

Consider education and training: Depending on the career you're interested in, you may need to pursue additional education or training. Research the options available to you and consider how you can gain the necessary skills and qualifications.

Create a plan: Once you've identified a career path you're interested in pursuing, create a plan to make it happen. This may involve taking courses, gaining experience through internships or volunteer work, or networking with professionals in the field.

Conclusion

Finding meaning in your work is essential for achieving lasting happiness, purpose, and success. By reflecting on your values, identifying your strengths, and seeking out opportunities for growth, you can find fulfillment in your job, no matter what you do. And if you've tried everything and still can't find meaning in your current job, don't be afraid to consider a career change. With dedication and hard work, you can pursue a career that aligns with your passions and brings you true fulfillment.

17: Pursuing Your Passion

Have you ever felt lost or directionless in life? Have you ever felt like you're going through the motions, but not really living? If so, you're not alone. Many people struggle to find their purpose in life and to pursue their passions. But the good news is, it's never too late to start. In this chapter, we'll explore the concept of pursuing your passion and how it can lead to lasting happiness, purpose, and success.

What is a passion?

First things first, let's define what we mean by passion. Your passion is something that you love doing, that brings you joy and fulfillment, and that you're willing to devote time and energy to. It's something that makes you come alive and gives you a sense of purpose.

Passions can take many different forms. It could be a hobby, such as painting or playing an instrument. It could be a career, such as teaching or writing. It could be a cause, such as animal rights or environmentalism. Whatever it is, your passion should be something that resonates with you deeply and that you feel called to pursue.

Why is pursuing your passion important?

17: PURSUING YOUR PASSION

There are many reasons why pursuing your passion is important. Here are just a few:

It brings meaning and purpose to your life. When you're doing something you're passionate about, you feel like you're living with purpose. You're not just going through the motions; you're actively engaged in something that matters to you.

It brings you joy and fulfillment. When you're pursuing your passion, you're doing something that makes you happy. You're not just doing it for the sake of making money or pleasing others; you're doing it because it brings you joy and fulfillment.

It can lead to success. When you're passionate about something, you're more likely to put in the time and effort necessary to succeed. You're willing to go the extra mile and to overcome obstacles because you believe in what you're doing.

It can inspire others. When you're pursuing your passion, you're living authentically and setting an example for others. You're showing them that it's possible to do what you love and to be successful at it.

17: PURSUING YOUR PASSION

How to discover your passion

So how do you discover your passion? Here are a few steps you can take:

Explore your interests. What do you enjoy doing? What hobbies or activities bring you joy? Make a list of everything that comes to mind, no matter how small or seemingly insignificant.

Reflect on your values. What do you care about? What causes or issues are important to you? Your passion should be aligned with your values.

Try new things. Don't be afraid to step outside of your comfort zone and try something new. You never know what you might discover.

Pay attention to your emotions. When you're doing something that you're passionate about, you'll feel a sense of excitement and joy. Pay attention to those emotions and use them as a guide.

Look for patterns. As you explore your interests and try new things, look for patterns. What activities or hobbies do you keep coming back to? What themes or values are present in your favorite activities?

Once you've discovered your passion, it's time to start pursuing it. Here are a few tips to help you get started:

Make time for it. If your passion is important to you, you need to make time for it. Schedule it into your calendar and treat it like any other important commitment.

Set goals. What do you want to achieve through pursuing your passion? Set specific, measurable goals to help you stay on track.

Find a community. Surround yourself with others who share your passion. Join a club, attend a workshop, or connect with others online who are also pursuing your passion. Having a community can provide support, accountability, and inspiration.

Learn and grow. Continuously learn and improve in your pursuit of your passion. Take classes, read books, and seek out mentors who can help you develop your skills and knowledge.

Embrace failure. Pursuing your passion isn't always easy, and you're bound to experience setbacks and failures along the way. Embrace these experiences as opportunities for growth and learning.

Celebrate successes. When you achieve a goal or make progress in your pursuit of your passion, take time to celebrate. Recognize and appreciate your hard work and dedication.

The benefits of pursuing your passion are many, but it's important to remember that it's not always easy. Pursuing your passion takes time, effort, and dedication. You may need to make sacrifices, face challenges, and deal with setbacks along the way. But the rewards of living a fulfilled, purposeful life are worth it.

In conclusion, pursuing your passion is an essential component of achieving true fulfillment in life. By exploring your interests, values, and emotions, you can discover what truly brings you joy and purpose. Once you've discovered your passion, it's up to you to make it a priority in your life and to dedicate yourself to its pursuit. Remember to embrace failure, celebrate successes, and continuously learn and grow in your pursuit of your passion.

18: Building Resilience and Grit

Life is a journey full of ups and downs, twists and turns, and unexpected challenges. Along the way, we may face obstacles that test our willpower, strength, and determination. Whether it's losing a job, experiencing a breakup, or dealing with a personal tragedy, these experiences can either make us stronger or break us down.

The key to overcoming adversity is resilience and grit. Resilience is the ability to bounce back from setbacks, while grit is the perseverance and passion to achieve long-term goals. Building resilience and grit takes time and effort, but it's a crucial component of achieving true fulfillment in life.

So, how can you develop resilience and grit? Here are some steps to get started.

Embrace your emotions

Resilience starts with acknowledging and accepting your emotions. It's normal to feel sad, angry, or frustrated when faced with a setback. Instead of trying to suppress these emotions, allow yourself to feel them. This will help you process your feelings and move on.

18: BUILDING RESILIENCE AND GRIT

Focus on your strengths

Identify your strengths and focus on them. Use your strengths to your advantage to overcome challenges. If you're good at problem-solving, use that skill to find solutions to your problems. If you're a good communicator, use that skill to express your thoughts and feelings to others.

Set realistic goals

Setting realistic goals is important for building resilience and grit. Break down your long-term goals into smaller, more achievable goals. Celebrate each small victory along the way, and use them as motivation to keep going.

Learn from your failures

Failure is a natural part of the learning process. Instead of dwelling on your failures, use them as learning opportunities. Ask yourself what you could have done differently, and use that knowledge to improve your approach next time.

Practice self-care

Self-care is essential for building resilience and grit. Make time for activities that make you feel good, such as exercise, meditation, or spending time with loved ones. Taking care of your physical and mental health will help you stay strong during difficult times.

Surround yourself with supportive people

Having a support system is crucial for building resilience and grit. Surround yourself with people who believe in you and support your goals. These people will provide encouragement and motivation when you need it most.

Practice positive thinking

Positive thinking can help you build resilience and grit. Focus on the positive aspects of your life, and reframe negative experiences as opportunities for growth. Replace negative self-talk with positive affirmations, and practice gratitude for the good things in your life.

Building resilience and grit takes time and effort, but it's worth it. By embracing your emotions, focusing on your strengths, setting realistic goals, learning from your failures, practicing self-care, surrounding yourself with supportive people, and practicing positive thinking, you can develop the resilience and grit you need to overcome any challenge life throws your way.

Remember, resilience and grit are not just about getting through tough times. They're also about pursuing your goals and dreams with passion and perseverance. With resilience and grit, you can achieve true fulfillment in life.

19: Setting Goals and Objectives

Have you ever felt lost or unfulfilled in life? Like you're just going through the motions and not really sure where you're headed? It's a common feeling, and one that can leave us feeling stuck and unmotivated.

But what if I told you that there's a simple way to break out of that cycle? That by setting clear goals and objectives, you can start living a life of purpose and fulfillment?

In this chapter, we're going to dive deep into the topic of goal-setting. We'll explore why it's so important, how to set effective goals, and the steps you can take to achieve them. So, let's get started!

Why Set Goals?

Before we dive into the specifics of goal-setting, let's first take a step back and ask ourselves: why bother setting goals in the first place?

For starters, goals give us direction. They provide a clear picture of where we want to go and what we want to achieve. Without them, we're just wandering aimlessly, hoping that we stumble upon something meaningful.

But more than that, goals give us motivation. When we have a clear objective in mind, we're more likely to take action and make progress. We feel a sense of purpose and drive that propels us forward.

And finally, goals give us a sense of accomplishment. When we achieve a goal, we feel a sense of pride and satisfaction that can't be replicated by anything else. It's a tangible reminder that we're capable of great things.

How to Set Effective Goals

Now that we understand why goals are important, let's talk about how to set effective ones. Here are some tips to keep in mind:

Start with the end in mind. Before you set a goal, take some time to envision what your ideal outcome would be. What does success look like to you? What do you want to achieve? This will help you set a clear objective to work towards.

Make it specific. A vague goal like "lose weight" or "make more money" isn't very effective. Instead, make your goal as specific as possible. For example, "lose 10 pounds in the next 3 months" or "increase my monthly income by $1,000 by the end of the year."

Make it measurable. Along with being specific, your goal should also be measurable. This means that you can track your progress and see how far you've come. For example, if your goal is to run a marathon, you can measure your progress by tracking your distance, pace, and time.

Make it realistic. While it's important to set ambitious goals, it's also important to be realistic. Don't set yourself up for failure by aiming too high. Instead, set a goal that challenges you but is still achievable.

Give it a deadline. A goal without a deadline is just a wish. Make sure to give yourself a specific timeframe to work within. This will help you stay focused and motivated.

Steps to Achieving Your Goals

Now that you've set your goals, it's time to start working towards them. Here are some steps you can take to ensure your success:

Break it down. Big goals can feel overwhelming, so break them down into smaller, more manageable steps. This will make it easier to stay focused and track your progress.

Create a plan. Once you've broken your goal down into smaller steps, create a plan for achieving each one. This might involve creating a daily or weekly schedule, or setting up a system for tracking your progress.

Take action. The most important step in achieving your goals is to take action. Don't wait for motivation to strike – just start working towards your goal, even if it's just a small step each day. Consistency is key.

Stay accountable. Find someone who can hold you accountable for your progress. This might be a friend, family member, or even a coach. Having someone to report to can help keep you on track and motivated.

Celebrate your wins. As you make progress towards your goal, take time to celebrate your wins along the way. This will help keep you motivated and remind you of the progress you've made.

Adjust as needed. As you work towards your goal, you may encounter obstacles or realize that your plan needs to be adjusted. Don't be afraid to make changes as needed to stay on track.

Examples of Effective Goals

Now that we've covered the basics of goal-setting, let's look at some examples of effective goals. These are specific, measurable, and achievable goals that can help you live a more fulfilling life:

Run a half marathon in 6 months. This goal is specific (running a half marathon), measurable (completing the race in 6 months), and achievable (with consistent training).

Save $5,000 for a down payment on a house in 1 year. This goal is specific (saving $5,000), measurable (within 1 year), and achievable (with budgeting and saving strategies).

Write a novel in 1 year. This goal is specific (writing a novel), measurable (within 1 year), and achievable (with consistent writing and dedication).

Learn a new language to a conversational level in 6 months. This goal is specific (learning a new language), measurable (to a conversational level), and achievable (with regular practice and immersion).

Complete a yoga teacher training program in 9 months. This goal is specific (completing a yoga teacher training program), measurable (within 9 months), and achievable (with dedication and commitment to the program).

In Conclusion

Setting goals and objectives is a crucial step towards living a fulfilling and purposeful life. By following the tips outlined in this chapter, you can set effective goals that give you direction, motivation, and a sense of accomplishment. And by taking consistent action towards those goals, you can achieve the life of your dreams.

20: Creating a Plan for Success

As humans, we all want to be successful in some way or the other. Success can mean different things to different people. It could mean achieving a certain level of financial independence, fulfilling a lifelong dream, or simply being happy with one's life. However, success doesn't just happen by chance. It requires hard work, dedication, and a well-defined plan. In this chapter, we will explore how to create a plan for success and achieve lasting fulfillment in life.

Step 1: Define Your Goals

The first step in creating a plan for success is to define your goals. What do you want to achieve? It could be anything from starting your own business to running a marathon. Once you have identified your goals, write them down and be as specific as possible. For example, instead of saying you want to start a business, write down the type of business you want to start, the target market, the revenue you want to generate, and the timeline for achieving this goal.

Step 2: Identify Your Strengths and Weaknesses

Knowing your strengths and weaknesses is crucial to creating a plan for success. Your strengths will help you leverage your skills to achieve your goals, while your weaknesses will help you identify areas that you need to work on. Be honest with yourself and list down your strengths and weaknesses. You can also seek feedback from your friends, family, or colleagues to get a more objective perspective.

Step 3: Create a Strategy

Once you have identified your goals, strengths, and weaknesses, it's time to create a strategy. This involves breaking down your goals into smaller, actionable steps. For example, if your goal is to start a business, some of the steps involved in this process could include market research, creating a business plan, raising funds, and launching the business. Write down these steps and set deadlines for completing each of them.

Step 4: Take Action

Creating a plan is only the first step. To achieve success, you need to take action. Start working on the actionable steps you have identified in your strategy. Don't wait for the perfect time or for everything to be perfect. Take action and make adjustments along the way.

Step 5: Monitor Your Progress

Monitoring your progress is crucial to achieving success. Regularly review your plan and track your progress against your goals. This will help you identify areas where you need to make adjustments and stay motivated as you see progress towards your goals.

Step 6: Stay Committed

Creating a plan and taking action is not enough. To achieve lasting fulfillment in life, you need to stay committed to your goals. This means persevering through challenges, staying motivated, and continuing to work towards your goals even when you face setbacks.

Step 7: Celebrate Your Successes

Celebrating your successes along the way is important to stay motivated and committed to your goals. When you achieve a milestone, take the time to acknowledge and celebrate it. This will help you stay positive and motivated to continue working towards your goals.

In conclusion, creating a plan for success requires defining your goals, identifying your strengths and weaknesses, creating a strategy, taking action, monitoring your progress, staying committed, and celebrating your successes along the way. With a well-defined plan, dedication, and hard work, you can achieve lasting fulfillment in life and unlock the secrets to true happiness and success.

21: Taking Action and Staying Motivated

Taking Action and Staying Motivated

In the pursuit of fulfillment, taking action and staying motivated are two key ingredients. The desire to achieve a fulfilling life is not enough; one must be willing to take the necessary steps to make it a reality. However, taking action is easier said than done. Many people struggle with the initial steps, while others may find it difficult to stay motivated along the way. This chapter will explore practical steps that one can take to overcome these challenges and move towards lasting happiness, purpose, and success.

Setting Goals and Creating a Plan

The first step towards taking action is setting goals and creating a plan. Without a clear idea of what you want to achieve, it can be challenging to take the first step. Goal setting helps to provide direction and purpose, while a plan helps to break down larger goals into manageable steps. Start by asking yourself what you want to achieve in life. What are your long-term goals, and what steps can you take to achieve them? Once you have a clear idea of what you want, start creating a plan. Break down your goals into smaller, achievable steps, and create a timeline for achieving each step. Having a plan in place can help to provide structure and focus, making it easier to take action.

Taking the First Step

Once you have a plan in place, taking the first step can be intimidating. Fear of failure, self-doubt, and procrastination can all get in the way. However, it is essential to remember that the first step is often the most challenging. Once you take the first step, it becomes easier to keep going. To overcome fear and self-doubt, focus on the benefits of taking action. Remember that every small step you take brings you closer to achieving your goals. If you find yourself procrastinating, try breaking down the first step into even smaller steps. For example, if your goal is to start a new exercise routine, the first step could be as simple as putting on your workout clothes.

Staying Motivated

Taking action is only half the battle. Staying motivated along the way is just as important. Motivation can be challenging to maintain, particularly when facing setbacks or challenges. However, there are practical steps you can take to keep yourself motivated.

Celebrate Small Wins

Celebrate every small win along the way. Recognizing progress, no matter how small, can help to keep you motivated. Celebrating small wins can also help to build confidence, making it easier to tackle more significant challenges.

Stay Accountable

Accountability can be a powerful motivator. Share your goals with friends or family members who can hold you accountable. Consider finding a mentor or coach who can provide guidance and support along the way.

Visualize Success

Visualization is a powerful tool for staying motivated. Take time each day to visualize yourself achieving your goals. Imagine how you will feel when you reach your goals, and focus on that feeling. Visualization can help to keep you focused on the end result, making it easier to stay motivated.

Take Breaks

Taking breaks is just as important as taking action. Burnout can be a significant obstacle to staying motivated. Taking breaks can help to recharge your energy and motivation. Consider taking short breaks throughout the day, or taking a longer break to rest and recharge.

Stay Flexible

Flexibility is key to staying motivated. Be prepared to adapt and adjust your plan as needed. Remember that setbacks and challenges are a natural part of the process. Rather than giving up, focus on finding creative solutions and staying flexible.

Conclusion

Taking action and staying motivated are two essential ingredients for achieving fulfillment in life. Setting goals, creating a plan, and taking the first step are critical to getting started. Staying motivated requires celebrating small wins, staying accountable, visualizing success, taking breaks, and staying flexible. Remember that the journey towards fulfillment is not a straight line, but a series of ups and downs. Embrace the setbacks as opportunities for growth and learning.

It's also important to remember that motivation can come and go. There will be times when you feel motivated and energized, and times when you feel discouraged and unmotivated. During the low points, it's essential to focus on why you started and the benefits of achieving your goals. Remind yourself of your purpose and vision.

Finally, don't be afraid to ask for help. Seeking support from friends, family, or a professional can help to keep you on track and motivated. Don't let pride or fear of judgment hold you back from asking for help.

In summary, taking action and staying motivated are critical to achieving lasting happiness, purpose, and success. Setting goals, creating a plan, taking the first step, celebrating small wins, staying accountable, visualizing success, taking breaks, staying flexible, and seeking help are all practical steps you can take to stay on track. Remember to focus on the end result, embrace setbacks as opportunities for growth, and never give up on your pursuit of fulfillment.

22: Overcoming Procrastination

Procrastination is something that many of us struggle with. We all have things we need to do, but sometimes we just can't seem to get started. We find ourselves putting things off, finding excuses, or just doing something else entirely. However, procrastination can be detrimental to our happiness, purpose, and success. It can lead to missed opportunities, added stress, and a sense of dissatisfaction with ourselves.

But why do we procrastinate? There are many reasons why we might put things off. Maybe we're afraid of failure or success. Maybe we don't feel confident in our abilities. Maybe we're overwhelmed by the task at hand. Or maybe we're just not motivated to get started. Whatever the reason, procrastination is something that we need to overcome if we want to achieve true fulfillment in life.

So, how do we overcome procrastination? Here are some strategies that can help:

Break it down

One reason why we might procrastinate is because a task seems too big or overwhelming. If this is the case, try breaking the task down into smaller, more manageable steps. Instead of thinking about writing a whole report, just focus on writing the introduction. Once you've done that, move on to the next step. Breaking a task down into smaller steps can make it feel less daunting and more achievable.

Set a deadline

Another reason why we might procrastinate is because we don't have a clear deadline. If there's no urgency to a task, we might keep putting it off. To overcome this, set yourself a deadline. Make it specific and achievable, and hold yourself accountable to it. Having a deadline can help you prioritize your tasks and make progress towards your goals.

Eliminate distractions

Distractions are a common cause of procrastination. If you find yourself getting sidetracked by social media, email, or other distractions, try eliminating them. Turn off your phone, close your email, and focus on the task at hand. You might find that without distractions, you're able to focus more easily and get more done in less time.

Find your motivation

22: OVERCOMING PROCRASTINATION

Sometimes, we procrastinate because we're just not motivated to get started. To overcome this, try finding your motivation. What's driving you to complete this task? What are the benefits of completing it? Focus on the positive outcomes and use them to motivate yourself to get started.

Use a timer

Using a timer can be a great way to overcome procrastination. Set a timer for a specific amount of time, say 25 minutes, and focus on the task at hand for that time. When the timer goes off, take a break. This can help you stay focused and make progress towards your goals.

Get an accountability partner

Having someone to hold you accountable can be a great way to overcome procrastination. Find someone who can check in on your progress, offer support and encouragement, and hold you accountable to your goals. Knowing that someone else is counting on you can be a great motivator to get started and keep going.

Start with something easy

If you're really struggling to get started, try starting with something easy. Choose a task that you know you can complete quickly and easily, and use that as a starting point. Once you've completed that task, move on to something slightly more challenging. Starting with something easy can help you build momentum and gain confidence.

Practice self-compassion

Finally, it's important to practice self-compassion. Procrastination can be frustrating and stressful, but beating yourself up over it will only make things worse. Instead, be kind to yourself. Recognize that procrastination is a common struggle and that it doesn't define you as a person. Treat yourself with the same kindness and compassion that you would offer to a friend who is struggling. Celebrate your successes, no matter how small they may seem, and be gentle with yourself when things don't go according to plan.

It's also important to remember that overcoming procrastination is a process. It's not something that happens overnight, and it's not always easy. But with patience, practice, and persistence, you can overcome procrastination and achieve true fulfillment in life.

In addition to these strategies, there are also some underlying factors that can contribute to procrastination. These include things like perfectionism, fear of failure, and low self-esteem. If you find that you're consistently struggling with procrastination, it may be worth exploring these underlying issues with the help of a therapist or counselor.

Ultimately, overcoming procrastination is about taking action. It's about recognizing that you have the power to make positive changes in your life, and taking steps towards achieving your goals. By breaking tasks down, setting deadlines, eliminating distractions, finding motivation, and practicing self-compassion, you can overcome procrastination and unlock the secrets to lasting happiness, purpose, and success.

23: Developing Discipline and Willpower

Introduction:

Discipline and willpower are two essential elements that lead to success and fulfillment in life. Without them, achieving one's goals and dreams can become nearly impossible. Discipline is the ability to control one's actions, thoughts, and emotions to achieve a specific outcome, while willpower is the ability to resist short-term temptations to achieve long-term goals. Developing discipline and willpower takes practice and patience, but the benefits are immense.

In this chapter, we will explore the different techniques and strategies that can help you develop discipline and willpower in your life. We will also discuss the benefits of having these two traits and how they can lead to a more fulfilling and successful life.

Part 1: Understanding Discipline

Discipline is often associated with punishment or strict rules, but it is much more than that. Discipline is about developing a habit of self-control and taking responsibility for your actions. It is about setting goals and making a plan to achieve them.

One of the first steps to developing discipline is to identify your goals. What do you want to achieve in life? What are your dreams and aspirations? Once you have identified your goals, you need to make a plan to achieve them. This plan should be broken down into smaller, achievable steps that you can take every day to get closer to your goals.

Another important aspect of developing discipline is to stay motivated. It's easy to get distracted or lose focus when you're working towards a long-term goal. To stay motivated, you need to remind yourself of why you're working towards your goals and the benefits of achieving them. You can also reward yourself for achieving small milestones along the way.

Part 2: Developing Willpower

Willpower is the ability to resist short-term temptations in favor of long-term goals. It's about delaying gratification and making choices that will benefit you in the long run. Developing willpower takes practice, but it's a skill that can be learned.

One way to develop willpower is to practice mindfulness. Mindfulness is about being present in the moment and observing your thoughts and emotions without judgment. By practicing mindfulness, you can learn to identify your triggers and cravings and develop strategies to resist them.

Another way to develop willpower is to create an environment that supports your goals. If you're trying to eat healthier, for example, you can remove unhealthy snacks from your house and stock up on healthy options instead. If you're trying to save money, you can automate your savings and avoid shopping for non-essential items.

Part 3: The Benefits of Discipline and Willpower

Developing discipline and willpower can lead to a more fulfilling and successful life. When you have discipline, you're more likely to achieve your goals and feel a sense of accomplishment. You're also less likely to be distracted by short-term temptations or negative influences.

Having willpower can also lead to better physical and mental health. When you're able to resist short-term temptations like junk food or procrastination, you're more likely to make healthy choices that benefit your body and mind.

Willpower can also help reduce stress and anxiety by giving you a sense of control over your life.

Conclusion:

Developing discipline and willpower takes time and effort, but the benefits are immense. By setting goals, making a plan, staying motivated, practicing mindfulness, and creating an environment that supports your goals, you can develop these two essential traits that lead to a more fulfilling and successful life. Remember that discipline and willpower are skills that can be learned and improved with practice. With patience and perseverance, you can unlock the secrets to lasting happiness, purpose, and success.

24: Embracing Failure and Learning from Mistakes

As human beings, we are wired to strive for success and achievement in all areas of our lives. Whether it's in our careers, relationships, health, or personal goals, we are constantly seeking to improve ourselves and reach our fullest potential. However, the road to success is rarely smooth, and failure is an inevitable part of the journey. In fact, it is often through our mistakes and failures that we learn the most valuable lessons and make the greatest progress towards our goals.

Despite this, many of us have a deeply ingrained fear of failure. We view it as a sign of weakness, incompetence, or even moral failing. We are afraid of what others will think of us if we don't succeed, and we worry that our failures will define us and limit our future opportunities. As a result, we often avoid taking risks, playing it safe, and sticking with what we know, even if it means sacrificing our true potential.

However, this approach ultimately leads to a life of unfulfilled potential and missed opportunities. If we want to achieve true fulfillment and success in life, we must learn to embrace failure and use it as a tool for growth and progress.

24: EMBRACING FAILURE AND LEARNING FROM MISTAKES

The first step in embracing failure is to shift our perspective on what it means. Rather than seeing failure as a negative outcome, we should view it as a necessary step in the learning process. Failure is simply feedback that tells us what didn't work and what we need to adjust in order to achieve our goals. By reframing failure in this way, we can remove the shame and judgment that often accompanies it and see it as an opportunity for growth and improvement.

The second step is to cultivate a growth mindset. A growth mindset is the belief that our abilities and intelligence can be developed through dedication and hard work. People with a growth mindset view challenges and setbacks as opportunities to learn and grow, rather than as a reflection of their inherent abilities. By adopting a growth mindset, we can approach failure with a sense of curiosity and openness, rather than defensiveness or self-doubt.

The third step is to practice self-compassion. When we experience failure, it is natural to feel disappointed, frustrated, or even ashamed. However, it is important to remember that we are all human, and that making mistakes is a normal part of the learning process. Rather than beating ourselves up for our failures, we should practice self-compassion and treat ourselves with kindness and understanding. This means acknowledging our emotions, validating our experiences, and offering ourselves support and encouragement.

The fourth step is to learn from our mistakes. Failure only becomes a true setback if we fail to learn from it. After experiencing a failure, it is important to reflect on what went wrong, identify what we could have done differently, and make a plan for how we can improve in the future. This process of reflection and learning is what turns failure into a valuable experience that can propel us forward.

Finally, it is important to take action and keep moving forward. Failure can be paralyzing, and it is easy to get stuck in a cycle of self-doubt and inaction. However, the only way to overcome failure is to keep pushing forward and taking steps towards our goals. This means setting new goals, taking calculated risks, and persisting in the face of setbacks and challenges.

In conclusion, embracing failure is a critical component of achieving true fulfillment and success in life. By reframing failure as an opportunity for growth and learning, cultivating a growth mindset, practicing self-compassion, learning from our mistakes, and taking action, we can turn our failures into valuable stepping stones on the path towards our goals. So the next time you experience a setback or failure, remember that it is not the end of the road, but rather a chance to grow, learn, and ultimately succeed It is important to note that embracing failure is not a one-time event, but rather an ongoing process. We must continuously work to shift our perspective on failure and develop the habits and mindset that allow us to learn and grow from our mistakes. This means practicing self-awareness, mindfulness, and self-reflection, as well as seeking out feedback and support from others.

It is also important to recognize that failure is not a one-size-fits-all experience. What constitutes failure for one person may not be the same for another. Our personal definitions of success and failure are shaped by a multitude of factors, including our upbringing, culture, values, and life experiences. As such, it is important to develop a clear understanding of our own goals and priorities, and to define success and failure in a way that is authentic and meaningful to us.

Another key aspect of embracing failure is learning to manage our emotions. When we experience failure, it is natural to feel a range of emotions, from disappointment and frustration to anger and despair. However, if we allow these emotions to control us, we can become stuck in a cycle of negativity and self-doubt. Instead, we must learn to acknowledge and process our emotions in a healthy way, and use them as a source of motivation and growth.

One effective way to manage our emotions is through mindfulness meditation. Mindfulness meditation involves paying attention to the present moment without judgment, and can help us develop a greater sense of self-awareness and emotional regulation. By practicing mindfulness meditation regularly, we can learn to observe our thoughts and emotions without becoming overwhelmed by them, and develop a greater sense of clarity and perspective.

Ultimately, the key to embracing failure is to recognize that it is not the opposite of success, but rather an integral part of it. Without failure, we cannot learn, grow, or achieve our fullest potential. By embracing failure and learning from our mistakes, we can cultivate resilience, creativity, and a sense of purpose that can propel us towards greater fulfillment and success in all areas of our lives. So the next time you experience failure, remember that it is not a reflection of your worth or potential, but rather an opportunity to learn and grow.

25: Celebrating Small Wins

As humans, we are wired to pursue success, happiness, and purpose in our lives. We set goals, make plans, and work tirelessly to achieve them. We envision ourselves at the pinnacle of success, basking in the glory of our achievements, and enjoying the fruits of our labor. But the reality of life is far from this picture-perfect scenario. The road to success is often bumpy, filled with challenges, setbacks, and failures. And it is easy to get bogged down by the weight of our unmet expectations and unrealized dreams.

This is where celebrating small wins comes in. Small wins are the little accomplishments that we achieve along the way as we pursue our goals. They are the milestones that mark our progress, the indicators that we are moving in the right direction, and the reminders that we are capable of achieving our dreams. Celebrating small wins is a powerful tool that can help us stay motivated, boost our confidence, and cultivate a positive mindset that is essential for success.

In this chapter, we will explore the importance of celebrating small wins, how to recognize them, and how to use them to propel us forward towards our goals.

The Power of Celebrating Small Wins

Celebrating small wins is a powerful way to boost our motivation and confidence. When we achieve a small win, it gives us a sense of accomplishment and validation that our efforts are paying off. It creates a positive emotional state that energizes us and encourages us to keep going. Small wins also help us to develop a growth mindset, which is the belief that our abilities and skills can be developed through hard work and dedication.

When we celebrate small wins, we are reinforcing the positive habits and behaviors that led to the accomplishment. We are also training our brains to focus on the positive aspects of our lives, which can have a profound impact on our overall well-being. Celebrating small wins helps us to develop resilience, grit, and perseverance, which are essential qualities for success in any area of life.

Recognizing Small Wins

The first step in celebrating small wins is to recognize them. Small wins are the little accomplishments that we achieve along the way as we pursue our goals. They can be anything from completing a task on your to-do list, learning a new skill, making progress towards a long-term goal, or overcoming a challenge. Small wins can be personal or professional, big or small, and they can happen every day.

To recognize small wins, it's important to set clear goals and track your progress. When you set a goal, break it down into smaller, achievable milestones. This will help you to see your progress more clearly and make it easier to celebrate small wins along the way. Keep a journal or a progress tracker where you can record your accomplishments and reflect on your progress. This will help you to stay motivated and focused on your goals.

Celebrating Small Wins

Once you have recognized your small wins, it's time to celebrate them. Celebrating small wins doesn't have to be a big or elaborate event. It can be as simple as taking a moment to acknowledge your accomplishment, sharing it with a friend or colleague, or treating yourself to something small.

Here are some ideas for celebrating small wins:

Share your accomplishment with someone. Tell a friend or colleague about your small win and share your excitement with them.

25: CELEBRATING SMALL WINS

Treat yourself to something small. It can be a cup of coffee, a favorite snack, or a few minutes of relaxation.

Take a moment to reflect on your accomplishment. Think about what you did well and how you can use that knowledge to achieve future success.

Write down your accomplishment in your progress tracker or journal. This will help you to see your progress more clearly and reinforce the positive habits and behaviors that led to the accomplishment.

Take a break and do something you enjoy. Celebrating small wins doesn't have to be all about work. Take some time to do something that makes you happy, whether it's reading a book, going for a walk, or watching a movie.

Reward yourself with a small goal-related treat. If your small win is related to a specific goal, reward yourself with something that will help you achieve that goal. For example, if you achieved a fitness milestone, buy yourself a new workout outfit.

Use your small win as motivation to achieve your next goal. Celebrating small wins can help you stay motivated and focused on your long-term goals. Use your small win as a stepping stone towards your next accomplishment.

The key to celebrating small wins is to make it a habit. Make a conscious effort to recognize and celebrate your small wins every day. This will help you to develop a positive mindset and stay motivated on your journey towards success.

Conclusion

Celebrating small wins is a powerful tool that can help us stay motivated, boost our confidence, and cultivate a positive mindset that is essential for success. By recognizing and celebrating our small wins, we can develop resilience, grit, and perseverance, which are essential qualities for success in any area of life.

To celebrate small wins, it's important to set clear goals, track your progress, and make a habit of recognizing and celebrating your accomplishments. Celebrating small wins doesn't have to be a big or elaborate event, but it should be something that makes you feel proud and validated.

In conclusion, celebrating small wins is a simple but powerful way to achieve lasting happiness, purpose, and success in life. By focusing on our small wins and recognizing our progress, we can stay motivated, boost our confidence, and achieve our goals with greater ease and joy.

26: Finding Balance in Your Life

Life is a constant journey, full of ups and downs, twists and turns, and unexpected surprises. Sometimes it can feel like we are running a never-ending race, struggling to keep up with the fast-paced world around us. We often forget to slow down, take a deep breath, and find balance in our lives. But achieving balance is crucial for living a fulfilling life. In this chapter, we will explore the importance of finding balance in your life and the steps you can take to achieve it.

What is Balance?

Before we dive into how to find balance in your life, it's essential to understand what balance means. Balance is the state of equilibrium between different aspects of our lives. It's the art of juggling all the areas of our life, including work, family, friends, hobbies, and personal time, without neglecting any one area. When we achieve balance, we feel centered, focused, and more productive. We are also happier, healthier, and more fulfilled.

Why is Balance Important?

Living a balanced life is essential for several reasons. First, when we are out of balance, we experience stress, anxiety, and burnout. We may feel overwhelmed, exhausted, and unable to cope with life's challenges. This can lead to physical and mental health problems, which can negatively impact our overall well-being.

Second, when we are out of balance, we are not able to give our best in any area of our life. For example, if we are working long hours and neglecting our personal relationships, our work will suffer, and our personal life will suffer too. We cannot be our best selves if we are out of balance.

Third, when we are out of balance, we miss out on the joys of life. We may become so focused on one area of our life that we forget to enjoy the other areas. For example, if we are working long hours, we may forget to take time to enjoy our hobbies, spend time with our loved ones, or just relax and enjoy life.

How to Find Balance in Your Life

Finding balance in your life is a process that requires effort, time, and commitment. It's not something that happens overnight, but with some dedication and perseverance, you can achieve balance in your life. Here are some steps you can take to find balance in your life.

26: FINDING BALANCE IN YOUR LIFE

Set Priorities

The first step to finding balance in your life is to set priorities. Determine what is most important to you in your life. Make a list of the areas of your life that matter most to you, such as work, family, friends, hobbies, and personal time. Then, rank them in order of importance. This will help you focus on what matters most and ensure that you are giving the necessary attention to each area of your life.

Create a Schedule

Once you have set your priorities, the next step is to create a schedule that allows you to give time to each area of your life. Plan your day, week, and month, including all your activities, tasks, and commitments. Make sure to schedule time for work, family, friends, hobbies, and personal time. By creating a schedule, you will ensure that you are giving the necessary attention to each area of your life and that you are not neglecting any one area.

Learn to Say No

One of the biggest obstacles to finding balance in your life is overcommitting. Many of us feel the need to say yes to every request or invitation we receive, even if it means sacrificing our own time and priorities. Learning to say no is essential to finding balance in your life. It's okay to decline invitations or requests that don't align with your priorities or schedule. By saying no, you will free up time and energy to focus on what matters most to you.

Practice Self-Care

Self-care is essential to finding balance in your life. It's essential to take care of your physical, emotional, and mental health to be able to give your best to other areas of your life. Take time for yourself every day, whether it's a few minutes of meditation, a relaxing bath, or a walk in nature. Make sure to get enough sleep, exercise regularly, and eat a healthy diet. When you prioritize self-care, you will feel more energized, focused, and productive in all areas of your life.

Set Boundaries

Setting boundaries is crucial to finding balance in your life. Boundaries are limits you set for yourself and others to ensure that your priorities and needs are respected. It's essential to set boundaries in all areas of your life, whether it's at work, with friends or family, or in your personal time. For example, you may set a boundary to not check work emails after a certain time or to not take work calls during family time. By setting boundaries, you will ensure that you are not overcommitting or sacrificing your own priorities for others.

Be Present

Being present in the moment is essential to finding balance in your life. When we are constantly thinking about the past or worrying about the future, we miss out on the joys of the present moment. Practice mindfulness and focus on the present moment, whether it's during a conversation with a loved one, a walk in nature, or a meal. By being present, you will feel more connected to yourself, others, and the world around you.

Evaluate and Adjust

Finding balance in your life is an ongoing process. It's essential to regularly evaluate and adjust your priorities, schedule, and boundaries to ensure that you are still aligned with what matters most to you. Take time to reflect on how you are spending your time and energy and make adjustments as needed. It's okay to say no to commitments that no longer serve you or to shift your priorities as your life changes.

In Conclusion

Finding balance in your life is essential to living a fulfilling and happy life. It's not always easy, but with some effort, time, and commitment, it's possible to achieve. By setting priorities, creating a schedule, practicing self-care, setting boundaries, being present, and evaluating and adjusting, you can find the balance that works best for you. Remember that finding balance is an ongoing process, and it's okay to make adjustments as needed. When you achieve balance, you will feel more centered, focused, and fulfilled, and you will be able to give your best to all areas of your life.

27: Prioritizing Your Time and Energy

Time and energy are two of the most valuable resources we have in life. They are finite, meaning that we only have a limited amount of them each day. How we choose to use our time and energy can make all the difference in our lives. In this chapter, we will explore the importance of prioritizing our time and energy and how to do it effectively.

First, let's define what we mean by prioritizing. Prioritizing is the act of organizing tasks, activities, and goals in order of importance or urgency. It means knowing what needs to be done first and what can wait. Prioritizing our time and energy is essential because it allows us to focus on what matters most and achieve our goals efficiently.

Why is it important to prioritize our time and energy?

When we prioritize our time and energy, we become more efficient and effective in our work and personal lives. By focusing on what matters most, we can achieve our goals more quickly and with less stress. We also become more productive and have more time for the things we enjoy.

27: PRIORITIZING YOUR TIME AND ENERGY

Here are some benefits of prioritizing our time and energy:

Increased productivity: When we prioritize our time and energy, we become more productive because we focus on what matters most. We get more done in less time, and we feel a sense of accomplishment.

Reduced stress: Prioritizing our time and energy can help reduce stress because we feel more in control of our lives. We don't feel overwhelmed by the endless list of tasks because we know what needs to be done first.

Improved focus: When we prioritize our time and energy, we can focus on the task at hand without getting distracted by other things. This improves our focus and concentration, making us more efficient and effective.

Better decision making: When we prioritize our time and energy, we make better decisions because we are not rushed or stressed. We have time to think through our options and make the best choice.

More time for the things we enjoy: When we prioritize our time and energy, we have more time for the things we enjoy, such as hobbies, family, and friends. We don't feel like we are constantly working or busy.

Now that we know why it's important to prioritize our time and energy let's explore how to do it effectively.

Step 1: Identify your goals and tasks

The first step in prioritizing your time and energy is to identify your goals and tasks. Start by making a list of everything you need to do, both personally and professionally. Once you have your list, group the tasks by category. For example, you could have categories for work, home, family, and personal development.

Next, identify your long-term and short-term goals. Long-term goals are those that take more than a year to achieve, while short-term goals are those that can be achieved in the next few months.

Step 2: Determine the importance and urgency of each task

Once you have identified your goals and tasks, it's time to determine their importance and urgency. Importance refers to how much the task contributes to your goals, while urgency refers to how soon the task needs to be completed.

To determine the importance of each task, ask yourself how much it contributes to your long-term goals. For example, if your long-term goal is to get a promotion, then a task that contributes to that goal, such as completing a certification, would be more important than a task that doesn't contribute to that goal.

To determine the urgency of each task, ask yourself when it needs to be completed. For example, if a task has a deadline, then it would be considered urgent.

Step 3: Prioritize your tasks

Now that you have identified the importance and urgency of each task, it's time to prioritize them. Start by focusing on the most important and urgent tasks first. These are the tasks that will have the biggest impact on your goals and need to be completed soon. Make sure to schedule time in your calendar to complete these tasks and give them your full attention.

Next, prioritize the tasks that are important but not urgent. These are tasks that contribute to your long-term goals but don't have a deadline. Schedule time in your calendar to complete these tasks as well, but don't let them take priority over the important and urgent tasks.

Finally, prioritize the tasks that are urgent but not important. These are tasks that have a deadline but don't contribute to your long-term goals. If possible, delegate these tasks to someone else or complete them quickly so that you can focus on the more important tasks.

Step 4: Manage your energy

In addition to prioritizing your time, it's important to manage your energy. Energy is the fuel that drives us and allows us to complete tasks. If we don't manage our energy, we can quickly become burned out and unproductive.

Here are some ways to manage your energy:

Take breaks: Take breaks throughout the day to recharge your energy. This could be a short walk, a stretch, or a few minutes of meditation.

Get enough sleep: Getting enough sleep is crucial for managing your energy. Aim for 7-9 hours of sleep each night.

Exercise: Exercise is a great way to boost your energy levels. Even a short walk or some stretching can make a difference.

Eat well: Eating a healthy diet can help manage your energy levels. Avoid processed foods and sugary snacks, and focus on whole foods such as fruits, vegetables, and lean protein.

Prioritize self-care: Self-care activities such as reading, taking a bath, or spending time with loved ones can help recharge your energy and improve your overall well-being.

In conclusion, prioritizing your time and energy is essential for achieving your goals and living a fulfilled life. By identifying your goals and tasks, determining their importance and urgency, prioritizing them, and managing your energy, you can become more efficient, effective, and productive. Remember to take breaks, get enough sleep, exercise, eat well, and prioritize self-care to manage your energy levels and achieve true fulfillment in life.

28: Practicing Self-Care and Self-Love

In today's world, where we are constantly surrounded by stress and chaos, taking care of oneself has become increasingly important. Self-care and self-love are the two pillars that make up the foundation of a fulfilling life. These two concepts are not just about taking bubble baths or getting massages, but about taking care of your mental, physical, and emotional well-being.

Self-care can be defined as any activity or practice that promotes physical, emotional, and mental health. It is a way of investing in yourself to improve your overall well-being. Practicing self-care can be challenging, especially in a fast-paced world where time is a luxury. However, it is essential to prioritize self-care to prevent burnout and promote a healthy lifestyle.

Self-love, on the other hand, is about accepting and loving yourself for who you are, flaws and all. It is about recognizing your worth and treating yourself with kindness and compassion. Self-love is not a destination, but a journey of self-discovery and self-acceptance.

28: PRACTICING SELF-CARE AND SELF-LOVE

Here are some practical ways to practice self-care and self-love:

Develop a self-care routine: Creating a self-care routine that works for you can help you stay consistent and committed to taking care of yourself. Your routine should include activities that promote physical, emotional, and mental well-being. Some examples of self-care activities include meditation, yoga, exercise, reading, taking a bubble bath, or going for a walk in nature.

Prioritize sleep: Sleep is essential for our physical and mental health. Lack of sleep can lead to fatigue, mood swings, and a weakened immune system. Make sure to prioritize sleep by creating a sleep-friendly environment and sticking to a regular sleep schedule.

Nourish your body: Eating a balanced and healthy diet can do wonders for your overall well-being. Make sure to fuel your body with nutritious foods that provide energy and promote good health.

Practice mindfulness: Mindfulness is about being present in the moment and fully engaged in the activity at hand. Practicing mindfulness can help reduce stress and anxiety, improve focus and productivity, and promote overall well-being.

Learn to say no: Saying no is an essential part of self-care. It is okay to say no to commitments that do not align with your priorities or values. Saying no can help you avoid over-commitment and burnout.

Surround yourself with positive people: Surrounding yourself with positive people can have a significant impact on your mental and emotional well-being. Spend time with people who uplift and support you, and distance yourself from those who drain your energy and bring you down.

Practice self-compassion: Self-compassion is about treating yourself with kindness and understanding, even when things do not go as planned. It is about acknowledging your struggles and failures without judgment and criticism.

Pursue your passions: Pursuing your passions can bring joy and fulfillment to your life. Make time for hobbies and activities that bring you happiness and fulfillment.

Celebrate your accomplishments: Celebrating your accomplishments, no matter how small, can help boost your self-esteem and confidence. Take time to acknowledge your achievements and be proud of yourself.

Seek professional help: If you are struggling with your mental or emotional health, seek professional help. Mental health professionals can provide support and guidance to help you overcome your challenges.

In conclusion, practicing self-care and self-love is crucial for achieving lasting happiness, purpose, and success in life. It is not a selfish act, but a necessary one to improve your overall well-being. Remember to prioritize self-care and self-love, and make them a part of your daily routine. By doing so, you will unlock the secrets to true fulfillment in life.

29: Cultivating Mindfulness and Gratitude

As we navigate through the ups and downs of life, it's easy to get caught up in the hustle and bustle of our daily routine. With so many distractions and demands vying for our attention, it's no wonder that we often feel stressed, overwhelmed, and disconnected from ourselves and others. However, there are two powerful tools that can help us stay grounded, centered, and focused on what truly matters: mindfulness and gratitude.

Mindfulness is the practice of being fully present and engaged in the present moment, without judgment or distraction. It involves paying attention to our thoughts, feelings, and sensations as they arise, and learning to observe them with curiosity and compassion. By cultivating mindfulness, we can become more aware of our habitual patterns of thought and behavior, and make conscious choices about how we respond to the world around us.

Gratitude, on the other hand, is the practice of acknowledging and appreciating the good things in our lives, no matter how small or seemingly insignificant. It involves shifting our focus away from what we lack or wish we had, and instead recognizing and savoring the abundance that already exists in our lives. By cultivating gratitude, we can cultivate a sense of joy, contentment, and satisfaction with our lives, even amidst challenging circumstances.

So how can we cultivate mindfulness and gratitude in our daily lives? Here are some practical tips and strategies to help you get started:

Start your day with intention: Before you even get out of bed in the morning, take a few moments to set an intention for your day. Ask yourself, "What do I want to cultivate in my life today?" Maybe you want to focus on being more patient, compassionate, or present with your loved ones. Or maybe you want to prioritize self-care and make time for exercise, meditation, or a hobby you enjoy. Whatever your intention, hold it in your heart as you begin your day.

Practice mindful breathing: One of the simplest and most effective ways to cultivate mindfulness is through the practice of mindful breathing. Take a few deep breaths, and then bring your attention to your breath as it flows in and out of your body. Notice the sensation of the air entering and leaving your nostrils, or the rise and fall of your chest and abdomen. Whenever your mind wanders, gently guide it back to your breath, without judgment or criticism.

Engage your senses: Another way to cultivate mindfulness is by engaging your senses in the present moment. Notice the colors, shapes, and textures of the objects around you. Listen to the sounds of the environment, from the hum of traffic to the chirping of birds. Pay attention to the tastes and smells of the food you eat or the beverages you drink. By immersing yourself in the present moment, you can cultivate a sense of wonder and appreciation for the world around you.

Keep a gratitude journal: One of the best ways to cultivate gratitude is by keeping a gratitude journal. Each day, write down three things that you're grateful for, no matter how small or insignificant they may seem. Maybe you're grateful for the sunshine, a kind word from a friend, or a delicious meal. By focusing on the good things in your life, you can shift your mindset from one of lack to one of abundance.

Practice random acts of kindness: Another way to cultivate gratitude is by practicing random acts of kindness. Whether it's holding the door open for someone, offering a compliment, or volunteering your time, small gestures of kindness can have a big impact on others, and can also help you feel more connected to the world around you.

Take a technology break: In today's hyper-connected world, it's easy to get caught up in the constant stream of notifications, emails, and social media updates. However, all of this technology can be overwhelming and distracting, making it difficult to cultivate mindfulness and gratitude. Try taking a break from technology for a set amount of time each day, whether it's 30 minutes or a few hours. Use this time to engage in activities that promote mindfulness and gratitude, such as reading, journaling, or spending time in nature.

Practice loving-kindness meditation: Loving-kindness meditation is a powerful practice that can help cultivate feelings of kindness, compassion, and gratitude towards ourselves and others. Find a comfortable seated position, and begin by silently repeating phrases of loving-kindness, such as "May I be happy, may I be healthy, may I be safe, may I be at peace." Then, extend these wishes to others, starting with a loved one, and gradually expanding to include all beings.

Cultivate mindful communication: Mindful communication

involves speaking and listening with intention and aware-ness, without judgment or reactivity. It involves being fully present and engaged in the conversation, and striving to un-derstand and empathize with the other person's perspect-ive. By cultivating mindful communication, we can build stronger and more meaningful relationships with others.

Reflect on your blessings: Finally, take time each day to re-flect on the blessings in your life. This could involve saying a prayer of gratitude, creating a gratitude jar or board, or simply pausing to appreciate the beauty and goodness in the world around you. By cultivating an attitude of gratitude, you can transform your perspective on life and unlock a deeper sense of fulfillment and purpose.

In conclusion, cultivating mindfulness and gratitude is a powerful way to unlock lasting happiness, purpose, and suc-cess in our lives. By practicing these skills on a daily basis, we can learn to stay present and engaged in the moment, appreciate the abundance that already exists in our lives, and build stronger and more meaningful relationships with ourselves and others. So take some time today to cultivate mindfulness and gratitude, and see how it transforms your life for the better.

30: Finding Fulfillment in Service and Giving

As human beings, we all strive to live a fulfilling life, one that is purposeful, joyful, and meaningful. We spend countless hours searching for that perfect job, that perfect partner, that perfect home, and that perfect lifestyle that will bring us the happiness and fulfillment we desire. But what if I told you that the key to true fulfillment in life is not found in what we receive, but in what we give? What if I told you that the path to lasting happiness, purpose, and success lies in service and giving?

It may sound counterintuitive, but the truth is that serving others and giving back to our communities can be one of the most fulfilling experiences we can have in life. When we take the focus off of ourselves and shift it to others, we open ourselves up to a world of possibilities, one that is filled with love, compassion, and generosity.

So how can we find fulfillment in service and giving? The answer lies in understanding the power of service and giving, and how it can transform our lives and the lives of those around us.

30: FINDING FULFILLMENT IN SERVICE AND GIVING

The Power of Service and Giving

Service and giving are two of the most powerful tools we have at our disposal to make a positive impact on the world around us. When we serve others and give freely of ourselves, we tap into our innate ability to connect with others and create meaningful relationships.

Service and giving also have a way of opening up our hearts and minds, allowing us to see the world from a different perspective. When we step outside of our own needs and desires and focus on the needs of others, we become more empathetic, compassionate, and understanding.

Furthermore, service and giving have been shown to have numerous physical and mental health benefits. Studies have found that volunteering and giving can lower stress levels, reduce depression and anxiety, and even improve physical health.

But perhaps the most powerful benefit of service and giving is the sense of fulfillment and purpose that it brings to our lives. When we serve others and give freely of ourselves, we tap into our true potential as human beings, and we find meaning and purpose in our lives.

Types of Service and Giving

There are many different ways to serve others and give back to our communities. Some examples include:

Volunteering: Volunteering is a great way to give back to your community and make a positive impact. Whether you volunteer at a local soup kitchen, animal shelter, or hospital, you can make a difference in the lives of those around you.

Donating: Donating to charity is another great way to give back. You can donate money, clothes, or other items to organizations that support causes you care about.

Random Acts of Kindness: Random acts of kindness are small gestures that can have a big impact. You can pay for someone's coffee in line behind you, leave a kind note for a coworker, or hold the door open for someone.

Mentoring: Mentoring is a powerful way to serve others and give back. Whether you mentor a young person in your community or offer your expertise to someone starting a business, you can make a positive impact on someone's life.

30: FINDING FULFILLMENT IN SERVICE AND GIVING

The Key to Finding Fulfillment in Service and Giving

The key to finding fulfillment in service and giving is to approach it with an open heart and a spirit of generosity. When we give freely of ourselves, without expecting anything in return, we create a space for love and compassion to thrive.

Furthermore, it's important to find ways to serve and give that align with our passions and interests. If you're passionate about animals, volunteering at an animal shelter may be the perfect fit for you. If you're passionate about education, mentoring a young person may be the best way for you to give back.

It's also important to remember that service and giving don't have to be grand gestures. Small acts of kindness can have a big impact on the world around us. Whether it's holding the door open for someone, paying for a stranger's coffee, or simply listening to a friend who needs to talk, every act of service and giving can make a difference.

Another key to finding fulfillment in service and giving is to approach it with a sense of gratitude. When we recognize the blessings in our own lives and the privilege we have to give back, we create a sense of abundance that allows us to give freely and joyfully.

Finally, it's important to recognize that service and giving are ongoing practices, not one-time events. Finding fulfillment in service and giving requires a commitment to making it a part of our daily lives. By making service and giving a habit, we can create a ripple effect of positivity and change that can transform our own lives and the lives of those around us.

Practical Tips for Finding Fulfillment in Service and Giving

If you're ready to start finding fulfillment in service and giving, here are some practical tips to get you started:

Identify your passions and interests. What causes or issues are you passionate about? What skills or expertise do you have to offer? Start by identifying the areas where you can make the biggest impact.

Find ways to get involved. Look for local organizations, charities, or volunteer opportunities that align with your passions and interests. Reach out to them and ask how you can get involved.

Start small. Don't feel like you have to make a huge commitment right away. Start with small acts of kindness or volunteering for just a few hours a week. As you become more comfortable, you can increase your involvement.

Make it a habit. Make service and giving a regular part of your life. Whether it's volunteering once a week or performing a random act of kindness every day, make it a habit that you commit to.

Stay open to new opportunities. As you get involved in service and giving, be open to new opportunities that may arise. You never know where your passion and expertise may be needed most.

Conclusion

Finding fulfillment in service and giving is not only a powerful way to make a positive impact on the world around us, but it's also a powerful way to find purpose, joy, and meaning in our own lives. By approaching service and giving with an open heart, a spirit of gratitude, and a commitment to making it a habit, we can create a life that is truly fulfilling and transformative. So why not start today? Take the first step on the path to fulfillment in service and giving, and see where it takes you.

31: Living with Purpose and Intention

Living with purpose and intention is a key component of true fulfillment in life. It is the foundation upon which we build our lives, and it is the driving force that propels us forward towards our goals and dreams. When we live with purpose and intention, we are able to align our actions with our values and beliefs, and we are able to create a life that is meaningful and fulfilling.

So, what does it mean to live with purpose and intention? At its core, living with purpose and intention means being mindful and intentional about how we spend our time, energy, and resources. It means having a clear understanding of what we want to achieve in life, and taking deliberate steps towards those goals. It means making conscious choices that are in alignment with our values and beliefs, and living in a way that feels authentic and true to ourselves.

Living with purpose and intention requires us to take a step back and reflect on our lives. It requires us to ask ourselves some important questions, such as: What do I want to achieve in life? What are my values and beliefs? What brings me joy and fulfillment? What impact do I want to have on the world?

Once we have a clear understanding of our values and goals, we can begin to live with intention. We can start by setting goals that are in alignment with our values and beliefs, and breaking them down into smaller, actionable steps. We can create a plan for how we want to achieve those goals, and make a commitment to ourselves to follow through on that plan.

Living with purpose and intention also means being mindful of our thoughts and actions. It means being present in the moment, and paying attention to how we are spending our time and energy. It means being intentional about the relationships we build, and the impact we have on those around us. It means being aware of the choices we make, and taking responsibility for the consequences of those choices.

One of the key benefits of living with purpose and intention is that it helps us to create a sense of meaning and fulfillment in our lives. When we are living in alignment with our values and beliefs, we are able to find joy and satisfaction in the things we do. We are able to find purpose in our work and our relationships, and we are able to feel a sense of connection to the world around us.

Living with purpose and intention can also help us to achieve our goals and dreams. By setting clear goals and taking deliberate steps towards them, we are able to make progress and achieve the things that are important to us. We are able to stay focused and motivated, even when things get difficult or challenging.

Of course, living with purpose and intention is not always easy. It requires a certain level of self-awareness and discipline, and it can be difficult to stay focused and motivated when we are faced with obstacles or setbacks. However, with practice and perseverance, we can develop the habits and mindset that are necessary to live with purpose and intention.

Here are some tips for living with purpose and intention:

Reflect on your values and goals. Take some time to think about what is most important to you in life, and what you want to achieve. Write down your values and goals, and keep them in a place where you can see them regularly.

166

Set clear goals. Once you have a clear understanding of your values and goals, set some specific, measurable goals that are in alignment with those values. Break those goals down into smaller, actionable steps, and create a plan for how you will achieve them.

Be mindful of your thoughts and actions. Pay attention to how you are spending your time and energy, and be intentional about the choices you make. Stay focused on your goals, and avoid distractions that are not in alignment with your values and goals.

Practice self-care. Taking care of yourself is an important part of living with purpose and intention. Make sure you are getting enough rest, exercise, and nourishing food. Take time for activities that bring you joy and help you relax, such as reading, meditation, or spending time in nature.

Cultivate positive relationships. Surround yourself with people who support and encourage you, and who share your values and goals. Build meaningful connections with others, and be intentional about how you spend your time with them.

Learn from challenges and setbacks. When faced with

obstacles or setbacks, use them as opportunities to learn and grow. Stay focused on your goals, and be willing to make adjustments to your plan when necessary.

Celebrate your successes. Take time to acknowledge and celebrate your achievements, no matter how small. Celebrating your successes can help you stay motivated and focused, and can give you a sense of accomplishment and fulfillment.

Living with purpose and intention is a journey, not a destination. It requires ongoing self-reflection, mindfulness, and commitment. However, when we are able to live in alignment with our values and beliefs, and take deliberate steps towards our goals and dreams, we are able to create a life that is truly fulfilling and meaningful.

So, take some time to reflect on your values and goals, and make a commitment to living with purpose and intention. You may be surprised at how much more fulfilling and meaningful your life becomes when you do.

32: Building a Support System

Building a Support System

As human beings, we are wired for connection. We thrive on social interaction and support from those around us. However, building a strong support system is not always easy. It takes effort, commitment, and a willingness to open up and share our vulnerabilities. In this chapter, we will explore the importance of having a support system, how to identify the right people to be part of it, and how to build and maintain those relationships over time.

Why Having a Support System Matters

There are many reasons why having a support system is important. Here are just a few:

Emotional Support: Life can be challenging, and we all face difficult times at one point or another. Having people in our lives who can provide emotional support can help us cope with stress, anxiety, and other difficult emotions.

Accountability: When we set goals for ourselves, it can be easy to give up when we encounter obstacles or setbacks. Having someone to hold us accountable can help us stay motivated and on track.

Perspective: Our support system can provide us with different perspectives on our problems and challenges. Sometimes, we can become so caught up in our own thoughts and feelings that we need someone else to help us see things more clearly.

Celebration: Our support system can also be there to celebrate our successes and accomplishments with us, providing us with a sense of validation and encouragement.

Health: Research has shown that having a strong support system can improve our physical health, lower our stress levels, and increase our overall well-being.

Identifying the Right People for Your Support System

Building a support system starts with identifying the right people to be part of it. Here are some qualities to look for:

Trustworthiness: You want to surround yourself with people who you can trust with your thoughts, feelings, and vulnerabilities.

Empathy: Look for people who are able to put themselves in

your shoes and understand your perspective.

Positivity: Positive people can help lift your spirits and keep you motivated, even during challenging times.

Shared Interests: People who share your interests and hobbies can be great candidates for your support system. You already have something in common, which can help to build a connection.

Diversity: It's important to have a diverse support system, with people from different backgrounds, experiences, and perspectives.

Building and Maintaining Relationships

Once you have identified the right people for your support system, it's time to start building and maintaining those relationships. Here are some tips:

Communication: Communication is key to any relationship, including those within your support system. Be open and honest about your thoughts, feelings, and needs.

Quality Time: Spending quality time with the people in your support system is important. Make time for regular phone calls, video chats, or in-person meetups.

Give and Take: Relationships are a two-way street. Be willing to give as much as you take, and vice versa.

Boundaries: It's important to set boundaries within your support system to protect your own mental health and well-being. Make sure you communicate your boundaries clearly and respectfully.

Flexibility: Relationships are dynamic, and they can change over time. Be willing to adapt and be flexible as the needs of your support system evolve.

Conclusion

Building a strong support system is essential for achieving lasting happiness, purpose, and success. It provides us with emotional support, accountability, perspective, and validation. To build a support system, identify people who are trustworthy, empathetic, positive, share your interests, and come from diverse backgrounds. Communication, spending quality time, giving and taking, setting boundaries, and being flexible are key to maintaining strong relationships. Remember, building a support system takes effort and commitment, but the rewards are well worth it. Take the time to invest in the relationships that matter to you, and you will reap the benefits for years to come.

It's important to note that building a support system is not always easy. Sometimes, it can be challenging to find people who meet all of the qualities that you're looking for. Other times, it can be difficult to open up and share your vulnerabilities with others. However, the effort that you put into building your support system is well worth it. The benefits of having people in your life who support, encourage, and challenge you are immeasurable.

In addition to building a support system, it's also important to remember that you can be a source of support for others. Be willing to listen, offer advice when asked, and provide a shoulder to lean on when needed. Remember, relationships are a two-way street, and giving support to others can be just as rewarding as receiving it.

Finally, it's important to remember that your support system may evolve over time. People may come and go, and your needs and interests may change. Be open to new relationships and experiences, and be willing to adapt as your support system changes.

In conclusion, building a support system is an essential step towards achieving true fulfillment in life. By identifying the right people, building strong relationships, and being willing to give and take, you can create a support system that provides you with emotional support, accountability, perspective, and validation. Remember, relationships take effort and commitment, but the rewards are immeasurable. Take the time to invest in the relationships that matter to you, and you will reap the benefits for years to come.

33: Overcoming Obstacles and Challenges

Obstacles and challenges are inevitable in life. No matter how well we plan and prepare, we will inevitably face setbacks and hurdles along the way. These obstacles can be frustrating, demoralizing, and even paralyzing. But with the right mindset, strategies, and tools, we can overcome them and emerge stronger, wiser, and more fulfilled.

In this chapter, we will explore some of the most common obstacles and challenges that people face, as well as practical and effective ways to overcome them. Whether you're struggling with fear, self-doubt, procrastination, or any other obstacle, this chapter will provide you with the insights, inspiration, and guidance you need to overcome it and achieve your goals.

The Power of Mindset

The first step to overcoming any obstacle is to cultivate a growth mindset. A growth mindset is the belief that you can develop your abilities and intelligence through hard work, dedication, and perseverance. It is the opposite of a fixed mindset, which assumes that your abilities and intelligence are fixed and cannot be changed.

Research has shown that people with a growth mindset are more resilient, more motivated, and more likely to succeed than those with a fixed mindset. They see obstacles as opportunities for growth and learning, rather than as threats to their abilities or self-worth. They are also more likely to take risks, embrace challenges, and bounce back from setbacks.

To cultivate a growth mindset, start by paying attention to your self-talk. Notice when you're using self-defeating language such as "I can't do this," "I'm not good enough," or "I'll never succeed." Replace these negative statements with more positive and empowering ones such as "I can learn this," "I am capable of overcoming this challenge," or "I will keep trying until I succeed."

You can also reframe your challenges as opportunities for growth and learning. Ask yourself, "What can I learn from this experience?" or "How can I use this setback as an opportunity to improve?" This will help you see your obstacles in a more positive light and motivate you to keep moving forward.

33: OVERCOMING OBSTACLES AND CHALLENGES

Overcoming Fear and Self-Doubt

Fear and self-doubt are two of the most common obstacles that people face. They can paralyze us, prevent us from taking action, and keep us stuck in our comfort zones. However, they are also natural and normal responses to uncertainty and risk.

To overcome fear and self-doubt, start by acknowledging and accepting them. Don't try to push them away or ignore them, as this will only make them stronger. Instead, acknowledge that they are there and remind yourself that they are normal and natural responses to uncertainty and risk.

Next, reframe your fear and self-doubt as opportunities for growth and learning. Ask yourself, "What can I learn from this fear or self-doubt?" or "How can I use this feeling as a motivator to take action?" This will help you see your fear and self-doubt in a more positive light and empower you to take action despite them.

You can also use visualization and positive affirmations to overcome fear and self-doubt. Visualize yourself succeeding in your goals and achieving your dreams, and repeat positive affirmations such as "I am capable," "I am worthy," and

"I can do this." This will help you reprogram your subconscious mind and overcome your limiting beliefs.

Dealing with Procrastination

Procrastination is another common obstacle that people face. It can be caused by fear, self-doubt, perfectionism, or simply a lack of motivation. However, procrastination can also be overcome with the right strategies and mindset.

To overcome procrastination, start by breaking your goals down into smaller, manageable tasks. This will help you feel less overwhelmed and more motivated to take action. Set deadlines for each task and hold yourself accountable for completing them on time. You can also use tools such as time-blocking or the Pomodoro Technique to increase your productivity and focus.

Another effective strategy for overcoming procrastination is to identify and address the underlying causes. Ask yourself, "Why am I procrastinating?" and be honest with yourself about the reasons. Are you afraid of failure or success? Do you feel overwhelmed by the task at hand? Once you identify the underlying cause, you can develop strategies to address it.

For example, if you're procrastinating because you feel overwhelmed, break the task down into smaller, more manageable steps. If you're procrastinating because you're afraid of failure, remind yourself that failure is a natural and necessary part of the learning process. Use positive self-talk and visualization techniques to boost your confidence and motivation.

Building Resilience

Resilience is the ability to bounce back from setbacks and adversity. It is an essential trait for achieving lasting happiness, purpose, and success. However, resilience is not something that you're born with; it is something that you can develop and strengthen over time.

To build resilience, start by practicing self-care. This includes getting enough sleep, eating healthy, exercising regularly, and taking time to relax and recharge. When you take care of your physical and emotional well-being, you'll be better equipped to handle challenges and setbacks.

You can also practice mindfulness and meditation to build resilience. These practices help you stay present and focused, even in the midst of chaos and uncertainty. They also help you develop a more positive and compassionate mindset, which can help you bounce back from setbacks and build stronger relationships.

Finally, seek out social support. Surround yourself with positive and supportive people who can offer encouragement, advice, and a listening ear when you need it. Building strong relationships is one of the most effective ways to build resilience and overcome obstacles and challenges.

Embracing Change

Change is inevitable in life, whether we like it or not. It can be scary and overwhelming, but it can also be an opportunity for growth and transformation. To overcome the fear of change, start by reframing your mindset.

Instead of seeing change as a threat, see it as an opportunity for growth and learning. Ask yourself, "What can I learn from this change?" or "How can I use this change as an opportunity to improve my life?" When you see change in a positive light, you'll be more motivated to embrace it and make the most of it.

You can also prepare for change by setting clear goals and

priorities. When you know what you want and where you're headed, you'll be better equipped to handle the inevitable changes that come your way. Stay flexible and adaptable, and be willing to adjust your goals and plans as needed.

Finally, embrace a growth mindset. Remember that you have the power to learn, grow, and adapt to any situation. Believe in yourself and your ability to overcome any obstacle or challenge that comes your way.

Conclusion

Obstacles and challenges are a natural and inevitable part of life. However, with the right mindset, strategies, and tools, you can overcome them and achieve lasting happiness, purpose, and success. Cultivate a growth mindset, embrace fear and self-doubt, address procrastination, build resilience, and embrace change. With these strategies in your toolbox, you'll be well on your way to overcoming any obstacle or challenge that comes your way.

34: Learning from Mentors and Role Models

Introduction

In the journey towards fulfillment, there is no doubt that mentors and role models play a significant role. Their influence can be invaluable in shaping our values, beliefs, and behaviors, helping us to unlock our potential and achieve our goals. In this chapter, we will explore the importance of mentors and role models in our lives and provide practical tips on how to learn from them effectively.

The Importance of Mentors and Role Models

Mentors and role models serve as beacons of hope, guiding us towards our aspirations and providing us with the necessary guidance to achieve our goals. They can be anyone, from a family member, a friend, a teacher, a boss, or even a celebrity. They inspire us, challenge us, and offer us a perspective that we may not have considered before. Their wisdom, experience, and insight can help us navigate the challenges that we may face in our lives and propel us towards success.

One of the key benefits of having a mentor or role model is the ability to learn from their experiences. Mentors have often already been through the ups and downs of life and can provide us with insights into what worked and what didn't work for them. They can help us avoid the mistakes they made and learn from their successes. This can save us time and energy, enabling us to achieve our goals more efficiently.

Another benefit of having a mentor or role model is the ability to gain new perspectives. They can help us see things from a different angle, challenge our assumptions, and expand our thinking. This can be particularly helpful when we are facing challenges or when we need to make important decisions. By offering a fresh perspective, mentors and role models can help us make better decisions and achieve our goals more effectively.

How to Learn from Mentors and Role Models

Learning from mentors and role models is not just about seeking out their advice and guidance. It's also about observing their behaviors and attitudes, studying their habits, and identifying the key factors that have contributed to their success. Here are some practical tips on how to learn from mentors and role models effectively.

Find a Mentor or Role Model that You Admire

The first step in learning from a mentor or role model is to find someone that you admire. Look for someone who has achieved success in the area that you are interested in, and who embodies the qualities and characteristics that you would like to emulate. This could be someone in your personal or professional life, or even someone in the public eye.

Observe Their Behaviors and Attitudes

Once you have identified a mentor or role model, start observing their behaviors and attitudes. Look for patterns in their actions, habits, and routines. Pay attention to how they communicate with others, how they approach challenges, and how they handle stress. By studying their behaviors and attitudes, you can gain insights into what makes them successful.

Ask for Advice and Guidance

Don't be afraid to ask your mentor or role model for advice

and guidance. They may be able to offer you insights and perspectives that you haven't considered before. However, be respectful of their time and don't expect them to provide all the answers. Remember that learning from a mentor or role model is a two-way street, and you also have to put in the effort to apply their advice and guidance effectively.

Learn from Their Mistakes

No one is perfect, and even the most successful people have made mistakes along the way. Learn from your mentor or role model's mistakes and use them as opportunities to avoid similar pitfalls. By understanding the challenges and obstacles that they faced, you can be better prepared to overcome similar challenges in your own life.

Emulate Their Habits and Routines

Finally, emulate your mentor or role model's habits and routines. Identify the key factors that have contributed to their success and try to incorporate them into your own life. This could be anything from their work ethic, their focus on personal development, or their commitment to a healthy lifestyle. By adopting these habits and routines, you can create a foundation for your own success.

Conclusion

Learning from mentors and role models is a powerful way to unlock our potential and achieve our goals. By observing their behaviors and attitudes, seeking their advice and guidance, and emulating their habits and routines, we can gain valuable insights into what it takes to be successful. Remember that learning from mentors and role models is not just about seeking their approval or validation, but about using their wisdom and experience to create our own path towards fulfillment.

35: Evaluating and Measuring Success

Success is a subjective term. What success means to one person might not be the same for another. Some people measure success by their wealth, others by their professional achievements, and still others by the quality of their relationships or the impact they make in the world. It is important to understand what success means to you personally and then evaluate and measure it accordingly.

Evaluating Your Success

To evaluate your success, you first need to define what success means to you. This requires introspection and self-awareness. Consider what makes you happy and fulfilled. What are your values and priorities? What are your long-term goals and aspirations? Once you have a clear understanding of what success means to you, you can begin to evaluate whether or not you are achieving it.

There are many different ways to evaluate success, depending on what is important to you. Here are a few examples:

Financial Success: If financial success is important to you,

you might evaluate your success by your net worth, your income, or the level of financial security you have achieved.

Professional Success: If professional success is important to you, you might evaluate your success by the level of responsibility you have at work, the number of promotions you have received, or the impact you have made in your field.

Relationship Success: If relationship success is important to you, you might evaluate your success by the quality of your relationships with your family, friends, and romantic partners.

Personal Growth: If personal growth is important to you, you might evaluate your success by the progress you have made in developing new skills, overcoming personal challenges, or pursuing your passions.

Measuring Your Success

Once you have evaluated your success, you can begin to measure it. Measuring success requires setting specific goals and tracking your progress towards achieving them.

When setting goals, it is important to make them SMART goals: Specific, Measurable, Achievable, Relevant, and Time-bound. This means setting goals that are clear, quantifiable, realistic, relevant to your overall definition of success, and have a specific timeline for completion.

For example, if financial success is important to you, you might set a SMART goal to save $10,000 within the next year. This goal is specific, measurable, achievable, relevant to your definition of success, and has a specific timeline for completion.

Once you have set your goals, it is important to track your progress towards achieving them. This means regularly reviewing your progress, adjusting your plan if necessary, and celebrating your successes along the way.

Tracking your progress can be done in many different ways, depending on what works best for you. Some people prefer to use a spreadsheet or other tracking tool, while others might use a journal or planner to keep track of their progress.

It is also important to remember that success is not always a straight line. There will be setbacks and obstacles along the way, and it is important to have the resilience and determ-ination to overcome them and keep moving forward towards your goals.

Celebrating Your Success

Finally, it is important to celebrate your successes along the way. Celebrating your successes helps to reinforce positive behaviors and keep you motivated towards achieving your goals.

Celebrating your successes can be done in many different ways, depending on what works best for you. Some people might reward themselves with a small treat or indulgence, while others might celebrate by sharing their successes with loved ones or taking a day off to relax and recharge.

Whatever form your celebration takes, it is important to acknowledge and appreciate the hard work and effort that went into achieving your success.

Conclusion

Evaluating and measuring success is an important part of achieving true fulfillment in life. By understanding what success means to you personally, setting SMART goals, tracking your progress, and celebrating your successes along the way, you can achieve the level of success that brings you true happiness and fulfillment.

However, it is important to remember that success is not a one-size-fits-all concept. What success means to you may be different from what it means to others. It is essential to evaluate and measure your success based on your own values and priorities.

In addition, it is important to maintain a balanced approach to success. Focusing solely on achieving success in one area of your life can lead to neglecting other areas, which can ultimately lead to a feeling of emptiness or lack of fulfillment.

For example, achieving financial success can be great, but if it comes at the expense of neglecting relationships or personal growth, it may not ultimately lead to true fulfillment. Therefore, it is important to evaluate and measure success in all areas of your life, and strive for balance and harmony between them.

Furthermore, it is important to recognize that success is not a destination but a journey. The process of setting goals, working towards them, and celebrating your successes along the way is what brings true fulfillment and joy. Therefore, it is important to enjoy the journey and not solely focus on the end result.

In conclusion, evaluating and measuring success is a critical step towards achieving true fulfillment in life. By defining what success means to you, setting SMART goals, tracking your progress, and celebrating your successes, you can achieve a sense of accomplishment and purpose in life. However, it is essential to maintain balance and harmony in all areas of your life, and to remember that success is a journey, not a destination.

36: Conclusion: Living a Fulfilling Life

Congratulations on making it to the end of this book, and thank you for taking the time to read through it. Over the course of the chapters, we've explored a variety of different concepts, strategies, and tools that you can use to help you achieve true fulfillment in life.

We started by exploring what fulfillment really means and why it's so important. We talked about how fulfillment is different from happiness, success, or achievement, and how it's really about living a life that is aligned with your values, purpose, and passions. We then delved into a variety of different strategies that you can use to help you uncover your own values, purpose, and passions, and to start living a more fulfilling life.

Throughout the book, we've talked about the importance of setting goals, creating healthy habits, and building a strong support system. We've explored the power of gratitude, mindfulness, and positive thinking, and we've discussed how to overcome limiting beliefs, fear, and procrastination.

At the heart of it all, however, is the idea that living a fulfilling life is a journey, not a destination. It's something that you need to work on every day, and it's something that requires ongoing self-reflection, self-awareness, and self-improvement. It's not always easy, but it is always worth it.

So, as you move forward from here, I encourage you to take what you've learned and to continue applying it to your life. Remember that fulfillment is not something that you can achieve overnight, and it's not something that you can buy or be given. It's something that you need to create for yourself, by living a life that is true to who you are and what you value.

Here are some final tips and reminders to help you on your journey towards a fulfilling life:

Stay true to your values: Your values are your compass in life. They guide your decisions and actions, and they help you stay on track towards a fulfilling life. Make sure that you're clear on what your values are, and that you're living in accordance with them.

Focus on what matters: It's easy to get distracted by the noise and chaos of everyday life, but it's important to remember what really matters to you. Take the time to reflect on your priorities, and make sure that you're spending your time and energy on the things that truly matter.

Cultivate self-awareness: Self-awareness is the foundation of personal growth and development. Make sure that you're taking the time to reflect on your thoughts, feelings, and behaviors, and that you're constantly learning and growing as a person.

Practice self-compassion: It's easy to be hard on yourself when things don't go according to plan, but remember that you're only human. Be kind and compassionate towards yourself, and give yourself the grace to make mistakes and learn from them.

Build a strong support system: Surround yourself with people who support and encourage you, and who share your values and goals. A strong support system can help you through tough times and keep you on track towards a fulfilling life.

Keep learning and growing: The journey towards a fulfilling life is a lifelong process. Keep learning, growing, and trying new things, and don't be afraid to step outside of your comfort zone.

36: CONCLUSION: LIVING A FULFILLING LIFE

Remember, living a fulfilling life is not a one-time achievement. It's a continuous journey that requires ongoing effort and commitment. But with the right mindset, strategies, and support, it's a journey that can lead to lasting happiness, purpose, and success.

Thank you again for reading this book, and I wish you all the best on your journey towards a fulfilling life!

Thank You

As we reach the end of this book, I want to say thanks for reading this book.

I want to get this information out to as many people as possible. If you found this book helpful, I would greatly appreciate you leaving me a review. This helps others find the book as well.

Disclaimer

This document is geared towards providing exact and reliable information in regards to the topic and issue covered. The publication is sold on the idea that the publisher is not required to render an accounting, officially permitted, or otherwise, qualified services. If advice is necessary, legal, financial, medical or professional, a practiced individual in the profession should be ordered.

This information is not presented by a financial or medical practitioner and is for entertainment, educational and informational purposes only. The content is not intended as a substitute for professional medical advice, diagnosis, or treatment. Always seek the advice of your physician or other qualified health care provider with any questions you may have regarding a medical condition. Never disregard professional medical advice or delay in seeking it because of something you have read.

The information provided herein is stated to be truthful and consistent, in that any liability, in terms of inattention or otherwise, by any usage or abuse of any policies, processes, or directions contained within is the solitary and utter responsibility of the recipient reader. Under no circumstances

DISCLAIMER

will any legal responsibility or blame be held against the publisher for any reparation, damages, or monetary loss due to the information herein, either directly or indirectly.

www.ingramcontent.com/pod-product-compliance
Lightning Source LLC
Chambersburg PA
CBHW060513130626
46553CB00002B/482

9798889131205